Contents

2   The Trophy *by Pat C...*

3   Welcomes from ...

5   Master plan to conquer the g...

9   Have-a-go heroes *by Peter Roebuck*

12   The World Cup XI from heaven *by John Woodcock*

16   Competition

20   Home is where the heart is *by Derek Pringle*

24   Cricket Live 99 *by Hugh Morris*

26   Not just here for the 'craic' *by David Llewellyn*

29   The tearaway with Anglo ambitions *by Andrew Radd*

33   A whole new ball game *by Jim Holden*

36   'Was' on the warpath *by Imran Khan*

38   Scotland does it for Love *by Bill Lothian*

40   Children's Competition

41   Flowers in full bloom for Zimbabwe *by Mark Williams*

45   Team biographies and statistics

115   Cricket World Cup Umpires

118   Cricket World Cup Referees

120   Cricket World Cup records and statistics

122   Sponsors page

123   The village green joins cricket's carnival *by David Hopps*

126   Cricket World Cup rules and format

128   Match Schedules

Official Cricket World Cup website:
www.ecb.co.uk/worldcup

PROGRAMME PUBLICATIONS

Programme designed and produced by
Programme Publications Group Ltd.
Tel: 01372 743377.
website: www.eventprogrammes.com.

Print and repro by
Linneys Colour Print Ltd.
Tel 01623 450450.

Editorial consultant: **Mark Baldwin**.

TERRORISM

We want today's match to be an enjoyable and successful event.
Help us to make things happen by:
- Keeping your belongings with you at all times.
- Informing a Steward or Police Officer immediately if you see anything suspicious.

If you are asked to evacuate the ground:
- Take all belongings with you.
- Listen to the advice given to you by Stewards and Police Officers.
- Leave the ground as safely and quickly as possible.

If you have any information about people or activities that could be linked to terrorist crime call the free confidential Hotline on 0800 789321.

The Trophy
by Pat Gibson

For the first time in the history of the World Cup, the 12 competing countries will be playing for a permanent trophy, designed and manufactured in London by Garrard, the Crown Jewellers, and valued at more than £27,000.

The World Cup trophy, crafted in silver and gilt, standing 60cm tall and weighing 11 kilos, features a golden globe held aloft by three silver columns. Its unique design ensures that it is instantly recognisable from any angle.

The globe itself is in the form of a cricket ball while the columns, styled as stumps and bails, represent the three essential pillars of the game - batting, bowling and fielding. Each column has the World Cup logo on the inside surface.

Inscription plates on the wooden base acknowledge the six previous champions - West Indies (1975 and 1979), India (1983), Australia (1987-88), Pakistan (1991-92) and Sri Lanka (1995-96). There is room for the next 12 champions.

The trophy was designed by Paul Marsden at Garrard who wanted to represent the equality of the teams taking part in the World Cup.

A team of craftsmen worked for two months, spending more than 500 man hours in the workshop, to create the spectacular finished article. The skills involved included fashioning the globe and pillars, engraving and gilding the globe and turning the wood for the base.

It will remain in the possession of the International Cricket Council but a replica, identical in every detail apart from the multiple inscribed plates, will be presented to the champions.

"This new permanent trophy is a symbol of the healthy state of cricket worldwide and our confidence in its continued growth," David Richards, chief executive of the ICC, said when he formally handed it over to Lord MacLaurin, chairman of both the England and Wales Cricket Board and the World Cup organising committee.

Apart from the trophy, the teams will be playing for a total of US$1million - the biggest prize fund the history of the game. The winners will receive $300,000, the runners-up $150,000 and the losing sem finalists $100,000 each.

The rest of the money will be split between the teams finishing in fifth and sixth places, the Super S qualifiers and ground match winners and losers.

Pat Gibson, a former cricket correspondent of The Daily Express and The Sunday Express, is now a freelance journalist who works extensively for The Times.

Welcome from the England and Wales Cricket Board

On behalf of the England and Wales Cricket Board, the organisers of the 1999 Cricket World Cup, I would like to extend a warm welcome to the competing teams, sponsors, suppliers and spectators alike. A welcome to what we firmly believe will be a wonderful 'Carnival of Cricket'.

This World Cup will feature more teams, more matches, re host venues and US$1 million in prize money which is re than three times that ever offered before. It will be the st extensive, colourful and widely-watched Cricket World p in history.

Twelve teams, 36 warm-up matches and 42 matches in tournament all add up to an unprecedented feast of cricket entertainment.

Organising a World Cup is a mammoth task with mind-wing logistics. Our decision to 'take the game to the ple' and to use 21 different host venues in five ntries magnified the task considerably. Three years of nning and an unprecedented demand for tickets ves us confident that the decision was right.

There is no doubt one-day cricket; with te ball and coloured clothing, has captured public imagination and presented us with opportunity to spread the game to a much ler audience.

The 1999 Cricket World Cup will introduce 'the w Faces of Cricket', new faces among the players, new es among the sponsors and suppliers and, most importantly, w faces among spectators.

Add to this a balanced mix of satellite and terrestrial vision coverage, which will take the World Cup to ndreds of millions wherever cricket is played, and the ievement of our goals is complete.

I thank our sponsors and suppliers, without whose port the tournament would not have been possible, and broadcast partners who will help us deliver the World Cup a vibrant, dynamic and exciting spectacle.

I also thank the small but dedicated group of manage-nt and staff of the ECB, whose sustained enthusiasm and lication will permit us to deliver what we are confident will the most successful Cricket World Cup yet.

Welcome to the Carnival and enjoy!

d MacLaurin
airman
gland and Wales Cricket Board

Welcome from the International Cricket Council

Now, at the doorstep of the Millennium, our glorious game has gone through its trans-formations in keeping with the changing wheels of time. After six World Cups, purists no longer scoff at the limited-overs version of the game, which now enjoys a peaceful co-existence with Test cricket.

The World Cup has also grown in stature since its inception in 1975. After the first three events were successfully hosted by England, the tournament moved abroad and has since been staged on the subcontinent in 1987 and 1996 and in Australia and New Zealand in 1992.

Along the way, the number of competing teams, spectators and television viewers has vastly increased, as have the exciting innovations of modern cricket such as coloured clothing, white balls and black sightscreens. The event comes home in 1999 bigger than ever, promising 300 hours of cricket over 42 matches, watched by 500,000 spectators and an estimated worldwide television audience measured in the hundreds of millions.

The 1999 Cricket World Cup will not only generate vital funds for the development of the game, but will also provide a wonderful platform for ICC's vision of a development programme, which will make cricket a truly global sport into the next century.

As the teams prepare to face each other, the individual battles will take shape - for runs, wickets and catches, for statistical achievements and financial rewards but, above all, for national pride and the chance of holding aloft the magnificent ICC Cricket World Cup trophy.

On behalf of the ICC, I extend the warmest of welcomes to all players, umpires, referees and other match officials and wish them all a successful tournament.

I convey the sincere thanks of all cricket followers to everyone at the England and Wales Cricket Board who have worked so hard for this gala event. Thanks also to the global partners, official suppliers and broadcasters without whose support the event could not be staged.

I am sure to see some enthralling cricket in the countdown to the final at Lord's on June 20. I wish every team the very best as they strive for the right to be called world champions of one-day cricket until we all meet again in South Africa in 2003.

Jagmohan Dalmiya
ICC
President

Your at-a-glance run rate reckoner.

Anything under this amount your/their team are stuffed.

Total score	Run rate required per over
100	2.0
110	2.2
120	2.4
130	2.6
140	2.8
150	3.0
160	3.2
170	3.4
180	3.6
190	3.8
200	4.0
210	4.2
220	4.4
230	4.6
240	4.8
250	5.0
260	5.2
270	5.4
280	5.6
290	5.8
300	6.0
310	6.2
320	6.4
330	6.6
340	6.8
350	7.0

Anything over amount your/th team are stuf

NatWest
We don't like cricket. We love it.

World Cu

National Westminster Bank Plc, Registered Office 41 Lothbury, London EC2P 2BP. Registered Number: 929027, England.

Master plan to conquer the globe

Dr Bacher believes that this Cricket World Cup will give greater impetus to the ICC's plans to popularise cricket in its developing nations.

The performances of Bangladesh, Kenya and Scotland in the 1999 World Cup will be watched with great interest.

If cricket is to thrive in the global sports market, it is important that the game becomes popular and is played to a high standard in more countries than is presently the case.

Spreading the game has been the task of the International Cricket Council's development committee, which was established by the ICC in July 1996 at the recommendation of David Richards, the chief executive, who pointed out that cricket was too narrowly based to compete effectively in the medium and long term with other more global sports.

As Mr Richards said: "Cricket must move on from being primarily a sport played in the Commonwealth to become a truly global sport".

The development committee, consisting of prominent administrators from various parts of the world, had five meetings, including two by telephone link-up, and visits were made to seven associate member countries, before presenting a report to the ICC in June 1997. This report has been the foundation for efforts to spread the game in the past two years.

Among the important developments has been the granting of official one-day international status to Bangladesh and Kenya, which has enabled these countries to compete at formal international level with the nine full member (Test-playing) countries of the ICC.

These countries will therefore arrive at the

David Richards, ICC Chief Executive

World Cup better prepared for the high intensity of competition against the best teams in the world. Scotland do not yet have full international status, but the ICC has been able to offer encouragement to Scotland, together with Ireland, Denmark and Holland, by facilitating tours to their countries by the A teams of Test-playing nations.

Performances in the 1999 World Cup will go a long way towards determining the number of teams and the format for the 2003 tournament in South Africa.

Twelve teams are competing in 1999. Kenya, Bangladesh and Scotland qualified by filling the first three places in the ICC Trophy tournament in Malaysia in 1997.

If Bangladesh and Kenya show they have improved their standards substantially, it would be an indication to the ICC that the strategy of granting official one-day international status was correct. A logical progression would be to grant such status to more associate member countries.

From a personal point of view, I would welcome the participation of as many as 16 countries in 2003 but it is crucial that playing standards are not compromised. One of the strengths of the 1999 Cricket World Cup is that

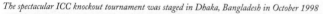
> *Blue print for a truly global sport.*

spectators and a global television audience will see a large number of highly competitive, exciting matches.

Only eight teams played in the first four World Cups. Both Sri Lanka and Zimbabwe played in the World Cup before becoming Test countries. It is to be hoped that other countries will use the tournament as a stepping stone to a higher status.

The World Cup is a crucial shop window for cricket because it will attract a television audience of hundreds of millions. One of the strategies of the World Cup organising committee has been to endeavour to ensure that television rights are made available to as many free-to-air television

stations in as many associate member countries possible. If new viewers are excited by what the see from England, it will be easier to promote t game.

After two years, the ICC development committee has made good progress. Landmarks include:

- A successful ICC knockout tournament was staged in Dhaka, Bangladesh, in October 19 which generated significant income for the development of cricket.
- The success in Dhaka has ensured that simila tournaments will be held every two years. Negotiations are in progress with the Disney corporation about the financial feasibility of t 2000 tournament to be held at Disneyworld Florida, USA, which would be a significant breakthrough into a vast potential market.
- A structure has been established. Ross Turner from Australia, has been appointed as the full-time development manager based in Londo Regional development officers are operating Europe, Africa, Asia, the Americas and, most recently, East-Asia Pacific. In the meantime, the Australian Cricket Board has done valuab work in investigating the potential for cricket

The spectacular ICC knockout tournament was staged in Dhaka, Bangladesh in October 1998

development in China and Japan.

Mr Turner has drawn up a five-year strategic plan which sets targets and timetables to increase participation by players, scorers, groundsmen and umpires in all associate and affiliate member countries.

The regional development officers have all been active. As an example, Nigel Laughton, the officer for Europe, organised 46 coaching visits and 13 umpiring courses in 1998 and was responsible for the distribution of 500 sets of soft-ball cricket equipment, as well as thousands of manuals, instruction booklets and posters. Coaching videos were translated into nine languages and distributed.

Sixteen countries competed in a successful Under 19 World Cup in South Africa in 1998. This will become a two-yearly event with the next event in Sri Lanka in January 2000.

In addition to broadening the base at grass ots level, the ICC development committee is mmitted to elite development, concentrating itially on assisting the leading associate embers to compete on equal terms in one-day

> *The Australian Cricket Board has done valuable work in investigating the potential for cricket development in China and Japan*

international cricket.

Bangladesh and Kenya have played in various one-day international tournaments over the past 18 months. Kenya, in particular, have achieved some promising results.

At the next level, Ireland and Scotland hosted Australia A in 1998 and will be visited by a team from South Africa during 1999, while Denmark and Holland played against India A in 1998 and will host Pakistan A this year.

I am pleased to say that this programme will be evaluated after the World Cup, with a view to organising tours to more countries, including USA, Canada and Bermuda. •

Ali Bacher, the managing director of the United Cricket Board of South Africa, will step down in June 2000, to take charge of the next tournament in South Africa in 2003.

Dr Ali Bacher with Nelson Mandela

digital made easy.

Have-a-go heroes

er Roebuck celebrates 25 years of
rious and spectacular World Cup action.

very four years the mightiest cricketers of
the age meet in some fortunate venue and
pit their skills against each other.
urally every player feels the tightening of
ve that accompanies these great occasions.
y know this is their chance to enter the
keting hall fame, even to join Pele and Keino
the other sporting giants in their separate
ld. It is an opportunity that may not come
n.

At the dinner beforehand these players will
around and see the famous men in flesh and
od. If they reach the final they will feel the past
ing around their boots as they walk through
Long Room. It'll be a time for men to deliver
performance of their cricketing lives, to
mon all their skills and experiences in one
assing effort. Some will succeed, others will
short, no-one will forget.

Of course, it all began as an adventure, almost
straction. It was appropriate that Australia and
West Indies met at Lord's in 1975 to fight for
title of the strongest one-day team around.
ese were the most powerful teams in the world,
the great men all played because limited overs
ket had not yet grown apart from its elder and
re restrained brother, had not developed tactics
temperaments of its own. Accordingly Dennis
ee and Jeff Thomson hurled the ball down
, later, amidst the mayhem, rushed up and
vn the pitch with typical Antipodean cheek.
d the West Indies were much the same, their
bowlers flat out and not a medium pacer
where.

Happily it was a glorious match, 60 overs a
e and not a circle in sight. Moreover, it was a
test dominated by its leading players, Clive
yd and his flashing blade wielded in a cat-like
nner by a hulk of a man, and Viv Richards

Clive Lloyd, peerless in 1975 (above)
Viv Richards, took charge of the 1979 final (below)

Kapil Dev... D'Artagnan

pouncing to run out various Chappells and half their congregation. As the shadows lengthened and Lord's came ablaze so the victors took their spoils.

Four years later the same Richards took charge of the entire tournament. He paraded himself, lauded himself, imposed himself, especially in the final where England could not contain his majesty. Meanwhile Collis King was slashing and cutting as if hurrying through a jungle towards some promised land. Not even Mike Brearley, the Merlin of the game, could stop this display of Calypso cricket, perhaps the last seen from the West Indians because they suffered elsewhere and hardened themselves against defeat. England started slowly and lost their champion, Ian Botham, as Richards ran a hundred yards to take a stirring catch. Perhaps it wasn't a hundred yards really but it seemed like it and, anyway, to suggest reporters colour their memories is like accusing a cat of drinking milk.

Nothing appeared more certain than a third West Indian triumph as the teams gathered again in 1983. By now the Sri Lankans had joined the fray, only to find most of their players hurried to hospital after facing Thommo himself. Upon reaching their destination the batsmen explained "Mr Thomson did it", and were asked whether they wanted to press charges. India had somehow reached the final, aroused by Kapil Dev's stirring 175 against Zimbabwe, arguably the finest rescue innings played in this competition. Kapil was D'Artagnan, saving a damsel in distress.

Few gave the Indians much chance in the final. But it was their day. They arrived to find Lord's in gloomy mood, buried under thick cloud. They managed to put a few runs on the board and promptly bowled and fielded like men possessed. Richards stood in their way, and it took a memorable catch from Kapil to remove him. Two hours later cricket's most populous land was celebrating its greatest day.

At last the Cup began its journey around the world. India and Pakistan buried their differences to stage the event. To their dismay neither reached the final, the tension proving too much. Nonetheless Eden Gardens proved a marvellous setting for the champions of England and Australia, and a tight match was widely enjoyed. In the end the Australians won, whereupon fireworks lit the skies and players past and present were paraded around the ground. It was a heady night and, perhaps, the best World Cup of them all.

> *By now the Sri Lankans had joined the fray, only to find most of their players hurried to hospital after facing Thommo himself.*

Next the tournament was taken to the lands of kangaroos, koalas and Kiri Ti Kanawa. By now the Zimbabweans and South Africans had joined the company and they played some rousing cricket. Meanwhile the gifted Pakistanis struggled along. Rescued by rain in Adelaide, they reached the semi-finals, almost despite themselves, whereupon Inzamam-ul-Haq played an innings of poise and power. New Zealand had fought a superb campaign, and Martin Crowe had captained and batted brilliantly. Taken as a

ection, Crowe's innings were the best seen in
World Cup. But it was not enough.
Pakistan met England at the MCG and
ʋed with such fortitude and spirit that they
ʋailed. Mushtaq Ahmed's googly, Wasim
ʋam's swingers and Inzamam's forceful hitting
linger long in the memory, as will the sight of
ʋe suddenly devout cricketers bowing to Mecca
n victory being secured. They did, though,
n displeased when their captain, the vaunted
an Khan, forgot to mention them in his speech.

> ❛ *One-day cricket has a life of
> its own and, nowadays, great
> players of its own.* ❜

Accordingly the Cup returned to the sub-
tinent with Sri Lanka invited to play its part
the first time. By now the competition had
ened considerably with Holland appearing,
bringing the tournament's oldest and youngest
ʋers, and Kenya also arriving and promptly
ʋting the morose West Indians in the University
n of Pune. More improbably the United Arab
ʋirates also won entry, whereupon their captain
ʋided to face Allan Donald without wearing a
ʋmet. It was not a pretty sight.
Sri Lanka played some thundering cricket to

Martin Crowe... most runs in a tournament

force their way towards the final, their openers
batting with panache and the middle-order men
playing resourcefully. Moreover their varied attack
bowled accurately and their fielding was athletic.

Arjuna Ranatunga proved a calm and poised
ringmaster. Sri Lanka survived the boycott of their
homeland, a riot in Calcutta and arrived in
Lahore ready to beat the Australians, with whom
their rivalry was keen. Not for the first time the
final produced a dazzling performance from a
great player, Aravinda de Silva playing the decisive
innings in a sumptuous display of correct batting.
Handicapped by a damp ball, the Australians
could not stop the ageing maestro and soon
another country was united in its celebrations.

Now it is time for new heroes to emerge. It
will be quite a gathering, a meeting of friends, and
all of them flourishing in the richness of their
game and the warmth of its crowds. Fifty over
cricket is here to stay. One-day cricket has a life of
its own and, nowadays, great players of its own. It
is, too, a democratic sport that gives every team a
chance. Someone will claim this hour, some will
take this day. Throughout there will be excitement
and a sense that something epic is close at hand. •

*Peter Roebuck, the former Somerset batsman and
captain, is now one of the most respected and
entertaining writers on cricket in newspapers and
magazines.*

n Khan... inspirational, but forgetful

The World Cup XI from heaven

Having watched the best at every World Cup, John Woodcock tackles the pleasurable task of selecting a team from players from the previous six tournaments.

Sanath Jayasuriya

The more alternatives, the more difficult the choice. Being asked to pick an eclectic eleven from players who have appeared in the previous six World Cups is to know that there was never more apt an aphorism.

The quarter century since this great quadrennial jamboree began may well have produced more strokemaking of a truly spectacular kind than any other in the history of the game. The golden age of batsmanship, celebrated nearly a hundred years ago, was more elegant, I don't doubt; but the game didn't girdle the earth then as it does now. Only Prince Ranjitsinhji had really shown what wizardry the Indians were capable of, and the Caribbean, like the sub-continent, remained a comparatively untapped source of cricketing talent. As for the Sri Lankans, it is only quite recently that they have had the chance to let the world know what wonderful natural batsmen they make; so wonderful, in fact, that I have chosen one of them, Sanath Jayasuriya, to go in first in this composite side of ours.

As Sri Lanka's opponents discovered to their cost in the last World Cup, there is simply no holding Jayasuriya if he gets his eye in, particularly during the first 15 overs of an innings, when nine of the fielding side have to be within the circle. Heaven help the captain who has to contend with the left-handed Sri Lankan at one end, batting as though a bowler's length and line counted for nothing, and Gordon Greenidge, with his bludgeon, at the other. Because it is limited-overs' cricket, Greenidge gets in just ahead of Sunil Gavaskar, Graham

ooch and that freest of spirits, Roy Fredericks.
Were it a five-day match, Gavaskar and
ooch might make the better opening pair,
avaskar with a Test record that speaks for itself
d Gooch as the best player in modern times of
t, short-pitched bowling. Greenidge though
ll go in with Jayasuriya, followed by Vivian
chards, the mightiest, most explosive attacking
tsman (*pace* Clyde Walcott) of the last 50 years.

> *Sachin Tendulkar, a batsman I dared to describe not long ago as being already as accomplished as Sir Donald Bradman.*

Because of the chances Richards and
yasuriya would be sure to take, an early disaster
two could not be ruled out. Who better to have
number four, therefore, than Sachin Tendulkar,
oatsman I dared to describe not long ago as
ing already as accomplished as Sir Donald
radman, although not, of course, as prolific.
chin has infinite concentration, the soundest of
ethods, great resilience and, for someone so
ort, extraordinary power.

With two marvellous all-rounders, Ian
otham and Imran Khan, at six and seven, the
oblem now is who to put at number five, as the
ane Warne

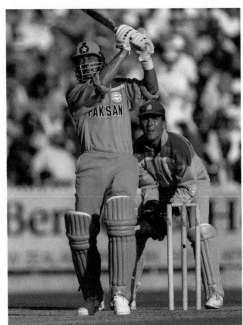

Imran Khan

last of the specialist batsmen. Here to be going on
with and in alphabetical order, are a dozen
candidates: Mohammad Azharuddin (India),
Greg Chappell (Australia), Martin Crowe (New
Zealand), Aravinda de Silva (Sri Lanka), Dean
Jones (Australia), Rohan Kanhai (West Indies),
Allan Lamb (England), Brian Lara (West Indies),
Clive Lloyd (West Indies), Salim Malik
(Pakistan), Javed Miandad (Pakistan) and Zaheer
Abbas (Pakistan). Genius and effrontery,
orthodoxy and intuition, wristwork and
inspiration, deftness and brute force, the rapier
and the broadsword, the East and the West – they
are all there.

I never saw a more dramatic last over than the
one in which Lamb pulverised the great Courtney
Walsh to give England a winning start to the
World Cup of 1987. It was at Gujranwala, some
50 miles north of Lahore, and so intense was the
heat, so extreme the tension, that both players had
to be helped off the field when the match
finished, Lamb with dehydration and Walsh with
mortification. But the 102 that Lloyd made as
captain of West Indies when they beat Australia at

Lord's in the very first World Cup final clinches for him that place in the order between Tendulkar and Botham. There was a force about Lloyd in that mood that was overwhelming, and when he failed with the bat his fielding was so boundless and athletic that he would still be in credit.

Nothing has had more to do with the raising, worldwide, of fielding standards than the introduction of one-day cricket. Many besides Lloyd, the king cobra, have thrilled us with their work in the covers: Derek Randall, Gus Logie, Roger Harper, Asif Iqbal, Keith Boyce, Alvin Kallicharran and the young Vivian Richards were among those who did so in the early days, and you will never see anyone better than Jonty Rhodes and Ricky Ponting, who are here now, playing for South Africa and Australia respectively. I would suggest there has never been a more dazzling ground fielder than Jonty; it is a tonic just to see him on the go.

> *Nothing has more to do with the raising, worldwide, of fielding standards than the introduction of one-day cricket.*
>
> Viv Richards

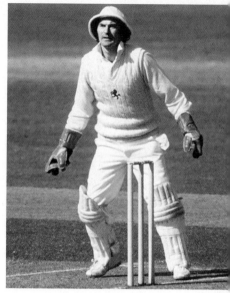

Alan Kn

So Lloyd comes loping in at number five, all six foot five inches of him; and then come Botha and Imran. I may have to walk into the city from the airport at Delhi when I go there next for not having found a place for Kapil Dev, for in the 1980s, when the world was rich in all-rounders, he bore comparison with all and any of them.

Apart from Botham, Imran and Kapil, there was also Richard Hadlee; but he comes into the picture in a minute. Not even Botham achieved anything more utterly startling in whatever sort of cricket, than the four successive sixes which Kap struck off Eddie Hemmings at Lord's to spare India from the need to follow on in the Test match there in 1990.

Alan Knott will keep wicket, not only for his brilliance and agility behind the stumps but because of the damage he could do with the bat and his irrepressibility. It came down to a choice between Knott, Rodney Marsh, Ian Healy and Jeffrey Dujon, all of them good for runs. Knott may need a net or two with Shane Warne, to become accustomed to the wiles and wonders of the incomparable Australian, who will be bowling as he did before his shoulder operation made a slightly more ordinary mortal of him. The left-arm spin will be entrusted to Jayasuriya, at the expense adly of Bishen Bedi. Abdul Qadir and Muttiah Muralitharan; two other great conjurors with the ball, would have been welcome additions too.

> **Yorkers with which Joel Garner used to shatter batsmen's toes and stumps with equal regularity.**

The field from which to choose the last two fast bowlers was almost impossibly wide. To some extent it was narrowed by the fact that the West Indians have rather had their wings clipped in one-day cricket by the regulation preventing them from bowling the short, rearing ball. Even so, we were still left with Dennis Lillee, Richard Hadlee, Allan Donald, Wasim Akram, Waqar Younis and Glenn McGrath, to mention only half a dozen. Not to have had a West Indian at all would have been ridiculous, and the yorkers with which Joel Garner used to shatter batsmen's toes and stumps with equal regularity made him a tremendous one-day bowler. So he and Hadlee are the two I have gone for, though it could just as well have been many others.

Of the final eleven, Imran Khan, Lloyd and Richards captained their countries in the World Cup. To win it for Pakistan in Australia and New Zealand in 1992 was arguably the defining achievement of Imran's career. For all that, I am inclined to think that our best captain would be Tendulkar, so to him goes the laurel. He has the game in his bones as incontestably as anyone I ever saw. He may be the smallest man in the side, but in other ways he is the tallest – and he has only just turned 25! What a talent; and what a constellation!

1	S T Jayasuriya
2	C G Greenidge
3	I V A Richards
4	S R Tendulkar (captain)
5	C H Lloyd
6	I T Botham
7	Imran Khan
8	R J Hadlee
9	A P E Knott
10	S K Warne
11	J Garner

John Woodcock was cricket correspondent of The Times from 1954 to 1987, and editor of Wisden from 1981 to 1986

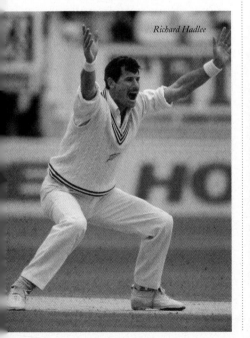

Richard Hadlee

Joel Garner

WIN an exclusive

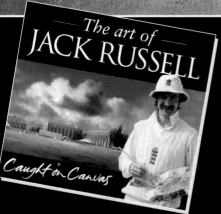

The art of
JACK RUSSELL
Caught on Canvas

Plus 6 runners up
prizes of special
NatWest edition of
'Caught on Canvas'

ack Russell print

of the winning moment of the 1999 Cricket World Cup

NatWest have commissioned Jack Russell to paint the winning moment of the 1999 Cricket World Cup at Lord's on 20 June, and you could win a print taken from the original by Jack Russell.

All you have to do is study the Jack Russell painting opposite and select from the list below which cricket ground it is:

A	OVAL		B	TRENT BRIDGE		C	LORD'S

Then write your answer A, B or C on a post card, or the reverse of an envelope, together with your name and address and send it to:
NatWest Jack Russell Prize Draw 1, Level 2, Glen House, Stag Place, London SW1E 5AG

All entries must be received by 4 June 1999

The winner will be the first name drawn from all the correct entries. The next six names drawn will each win a special NatWest edition of 'Caught on Canvas', the definitive book of Jack Russell and his paintings.

There will be another opportunity to win these prizes at the Super Six Semi-final and Final stages of the competition.

Be Part of the Carnival

ICC Cricket
World Cup
England 99

Home is where the heart is

Kenya-born Derek Pringle has no doubt which team he will be supporting.

Derek Pringle

W hen it comes to supporting England at cricket, I'm afraid I occasionally fail the "Tebbitt test." As a former player whose 30 Tests and two World Cups were played wearing three lions on my chest, my days of treachery will be limited to just one. May 18 – the day England play Kenya at Canterbury.

Cool Britannia may well rule, but with the World Cup involving 12 teams from around the globe, I daresay I will not be the only Briton to fall short of storming Norman's yardstick of unconditional support for England. Indeed, if Kenya can spring a surprise against Alec Stewart's side, as they did during the last World Cup when they beat the West Indies in Pune, I shall be the first to party. No matter how hard you try, you cannot take Africa out of the boy.

Of course, I blame it on my childhood which probably suffered from being too idyllic. Growing up, especially where sport is concerned, is the time when powerful and lasting allegiances are made and Kenya had a magic that further deepened the etching process.

In fact, playing cricket was just one of the many pleasures afforded by a climate perfect for year-round indulgence of the great outdoors. I'd probably seen the Big Five – lion, leopard, rhino, elephant and buffalo – before I took five-for on the cricket field.

In my case, it wasn't just the weather that helped nurture my passion. My father Donald, a staunch Lancashire supporter and a fine cricketer who played in the inaugural World Cup in 1975 for East Africa (of which Kenya was then a part), was also a major factor. Sadly, he died some 12 years before I made my World Cup ut for England.

As cricketing educations go, it was unusual.
k then, the pitches almost exclusively
sisted of coir or jute mats, stretched tight
r a firm murram (compacted gravel) base.
rely repaying out and out pace, they instead
ced budding fast bowlers into exploring swing
d cut. Nairobi is over 5,000 feet above sea level
d two-piece balls were preferred. Four piecers,
standard used in first-class cricket, tended
t to move off the straight at altitude.

Nowadays, most of the pitches are turf,
ough without a single heavy roller to be found
the country, the surfaces tend to be slow and
v. Once again fast bowling is rarely rewarded,
ich is a shame because both Martin and Tony
ji, as well as Thomas Odoyo and Joseph
gara, all have the ability to bowl quickly.

Although primarily a swing bowler like my
ther, my best ever performance came when
wling wrist-spin at the Rift Valley sports club
Nakuru, a market town some 100 miles north
the capital. Somehow – I recall at least five
tches being dropped off bowlers at the other
d – all ten wickets fell to me, a feat that
sured victory for Nairobi Schools under
irteen and a halves over the Up-Country
uivalent.

Maurice Odumbe

> **It has been gratifying to see how cricket there has progressed in unexpected and pleasing ways.**

Since leaving Kenya for good in 1976, it has
een gratifying to see how cricket there has
rogressed in unexpected and pleasing ways. For
arters, eight of the present 15-man squad are
frican; an amazing proportion given that only
ne, a Ugandan, was playing the game during
y time at secondary school.

Perhaps even more astounding is that seven
f the eight hail from the Luo and Abaluhya
ibes in Nyanza province, an area squashed in
etween the western edge of the great Rift Valley
nd the eastern shore of Lake Victoria. It is a
lace that probably last saw cricket when the old

District Commissioner put out a team, some 20 years before any of today's crop of tyros were even born.

So where have Maurice Odumbe, Steve Tikolo, Kennedy Otieno and the Sujis suddenly appeared from? What inspired them when the rest of the country's youth seemed to prefer anything but cricket?

Well, according to stalwarts involved in Kenya cricket, like Harilal Shah and Jasmer Singh, they simply picked up the game as kids by watching net practice at the Sir Ali sports club in Nairobi, a club adjacent to the houses their parents lived in.

What the largely Muslim players at the club noticed was that the boys would set up their own impromptu game afterwards, using sticks for bats, dustbins for wickets and dried corn cobs as balls. However, such was their enthusiasm and skill, that it wasn't long before they were asked to join in and a full conversion was made. If it all sounds rather fanciful, the evidence is concrete, and Kenya now boast a 20-man squad of full-time professionals.

If the move to professionalism suggests a country making its way into the game, it should be remembered that cricket is not a recent phenomenon in these parts. In fact the first cricket match was played during 1896 in Mombasa, when the country was a British colony.

Once the interior was thought habitable, the game spread to other parts, the process more linear than osmotic, relying on the tortuous progress of the famous "lunatic-line" from Mombasa to Lake Victoria for its germination. Just how many promising wrist-spinners the man-eating lions of Tsavo consumed will never be known.

The railway was built mainly by indentured Indian labour, which, bringing their families with them, later settled in Nairobi and Mombasa, the only places where cricket leagues now exist. It was these communities, Hindus, Muslims and Ismaelis, along with the white settlers, who were instrumental in creating the wealth of clubs that grew up in the pre-independence era.

Kennedy Otieno in action against Australia

> ❛ *Just how many promising wrist-spinners the man-eating Lions of Tsavo consumed will never be known.* ❜

Although today's sticklers for political correctness would baulk at the thought of it, the annual European v Asian encounters were the "Test" matches of their day. Highly competitive, they attracted large vociferous crowds and, apart from the agricultural show, were the premier event on the social calendar. At the time, the local African viewed cricket with a mixture of puzzlement and indifference.

After independence in 1963, it was Kenya's athletes, especially their distance runners, who began to gain international recognition.

Kipchoge Keino, Amos Biwott and Naftali Temu all won Olympic gold in Mexico. Their influence, along with that of football, made popular by its simplicity and portability, largely won over the black population.

Once Britain had dismantled its colonial machine in the 60's, cricket really needed to attract the African to keep its critical mass. Unfortunately, it has only been in the last 10-15 years that this has happened and only then on a minute scale.

The omens for the new millennium are good though, and high interest levels in schools are being supplemented by youth schemes set up by the top ten league clubs. Unfortunately, terrestrial television, that fast-tracker of trends, will not be showing Kenya's World Cup matches, which will only be available via satellite TV, a luxury only the wealthy minority can afford.

Taking the necessary leaps has not been easy but fortunately, Kenya Breweries, no doubt sensing strong competition from South African beer, have decided to sponsor the squad to the tune of 30 million shillings (about £300,000)

r the next five years. It is a decent sized pot
d one that also helped to secure the services of
: former West Indian Test player, Alvin
llicharran, the current head coach.

> *Kenya are a confident outfit who
> show plenty of cricketing nous and
> field brilliantly.* **'**

Depending on seniority, the players are paid
tween 300 and 600 pounds a month, a sum
at dispenses with the need for a job, and
stead allows them to train and practise five
ys a week.

This freedom has paid off and a recent
CC touring side – containing nine current
unty professionals, including Matthew
aynard, Ed Giddins and Richard Illingworth –
s trounced 4-0 in one-day matches. According
Hampshire's John Stephenson, a member of
e vanquished MCC side, Kenya are a confident
tfit who show plenty of cricketing nous and
ld brilliantly.

The squad is well balanced and has a glut of
all-rounders. Captained by left-arm spinner Asif
Karim, a former national tennis champion, they
have a depth if not a cutting edge. In particular,
watch out for Mohammed Sheikh, an exciting
teenager, and Tom Odoyo, 21, a potential
African Botham.

Giant killers tend to live on in the mind and
Kenya will want to slay their quota this time.
Their goal of achieving Test status within five
years needs high profile trophies and this World
Cup offers them ample opportunity.

Despite their inexperience over the longer
game, Kenya have never lacked ambition. If the
seed sowing in schools can continue, and
government recognition is forthcoming, then
those deep azure African skies are the limit.
Soon, perhaps, Test matches, as well as the big
five, will be seen near the Equator. •

*Derek Pringle, the former Essex and England
all-rounder, is cricket correspondent of
The Independent*

Kenyan batsman, Hitesh Modi

Cricket Live 99

by Hugh Morris

When I took over from Micky Stewart as the ECB's Technical Director at the end of 1997, I was keen to raise the profile of cricket coaches still further and make our coaching base the envy of other countries.

This summer the technical department will take a significant step towards achieving that goal by staging Cricket Live 99 - the World Cricket Coaches Conference and Exhibition at the NEC in Birmingham on June 1 and 2.

Featuring famous cricket names such as Sir Richard Hadlee, Allan Donald, Bob Woolmer, Desmond Haynes, Jonty Rhodes, Clive Rice, Graham Gooch, Terry Jenner and Bob Taylor, the event is a world first and we expect it will attract coaches from home and abroad.

Sponsored by Rover, Cricket Live 99 will focus on the needs of players and coaches involved in cricket at all levels and in all areas - from schools to first class clubs, from coaching to purchasing equipment, from the playground to the Test arena.

Scheduled to take place in between the group stage and the Super Six stage of the World Cup, we believe it will provide an invaluable networking and marketing opportunity for everyone involved in the game.

We have included sessions on all disciplines of the game and have also incorporated important aspects of sports science.

The event programme is wide-ranging and includes:

- Master classes and coaching sessions on all aspects of the game in the NEC Arena by star players and coaches.
- The ECB's Kwik Cricket Roadshow sponsored by Vodafone.

Allan Donald (above)   *Jonty Rhodes*

In-depth workshops and lectures on all aspects of the game including leadership and captaincy, psychology, bio-mechanics and fitness.

Demonstrations of the latest innovations in cricket coaching aids and equipment.

Any cricket coach who wants to pick up tips a preparation and training from some of the me's biggest names will be spoilt for choice. he highlights of the conference programme clude sessions on the art of leg-spin bowling by nner, Shane Warne's coach; practical tips for ick-bowling by Hadlee, a demonstration of elding drills by the legendary South frican Rhodes and a wicket-keeping asterclass by the former England and erbyshire wicketkeeper Taylor.

The seminar programme is equally citing. Among those taking part are rmer South African captain Rice - w the new director of cricket at ottinghamshire - who will take a ssion on leadership skills; tai-chi pert Mark Sheppard and England 17 coach Tim Boon who will reveal w movement, balance and breathing n aid cricketers and South Africa's onald who will take part in a Q and A session out fast bowling.

It all adds up to the most ambitious project e technical department has undertaken so far d I am indebted to my colleague Gordon ord, the ECB's National Coach Education o-ordinator, for coming up with the original ea.

To date, the event has met with an thusiastic response from cricket coaches ationwide and we are also targeting teachers, udent teachers and people working in the ealth and leisure industries.

We believe that it will act as a focal point for e cricket world and feel confident it will leave lasting legacy from which future generations of icketers will benefit

In addition to planning for Cricket Live 99, the technical department will be rolling out the revamped and expanded Rover Cricket Coach Initiative this summer.

Currently, there are more than 30,000 qualified cricket coaches nationwide with around 2,000 qualifying every year through the Rover scheme.

The new five-stage scheme, which Rover have agreed to sponsor for a further two years, is designed to equip coaches with the skills to progress all the way from the playground to the Test arena. Richie Richardson, Graham Gooch and Mike Gatting are among those who have signed up for the scheme to date.

The revamped scheme focuses on the development of technique, tactics, mental discipline, physical fitness and lifestyle management - a far wider remit than the original National Coaching Scheme which was first drafted in 1952 and has remained largely the same ever since.

The current scheme has proved extremely successful in producing large numbers of coaches able to work with cricketers at junior and recreational level. The challenge facing the technical department now is to improve on the quality of coaching available, particularly at international level.

Cricket Live 99 is an integral part of this process and we believe it will provide a fascinating and enthralling two days for anyone keen to develop their coaching skills. So if you want to pick up a few tips from Messrs Haynes, Rice, Hadlee or Rhodes on any aspect of the game - get in touch with our event organising team now.

Anyone wishing to register to their interest in visiting or exhibiting at the event should either phone the Edgbaston office of the ECB on 0121 440 1748 (fax 0121 446 6344) or the Event Management team on 01926 888123 (fax 01926 888004).

Not just here for the 'craic'

Cricket's first international match was staged in Ireland. Nearly 150 years later the Irish finally compete in the World Cup. David Llewellyn reports.

There is no doubt in which direction Irish cricket is looking, and that is forward. Indeed any mention of Ireland's historic victory over West Indies in Londonderry in 1969 is likely to elicit a groan. "We need to forget about Sion Mills," says Robin Walsh, the Irish Cricket Union's spokesman.

And the fact that it is West Indies who were drawn to play at Clontarf in Dublin against Bangladesh in this year's World Cup is pure coincidence. That it is not an Ireland side who will take the field is probably hard to swallow for some.

But the appointment almost four years ago of former England, Derbyshire and Nottinghamshire pace bowler Mike Hendrick as the first full-time national coach has gone a long way to establishing not only Ireland's credibility within the international cricket community, but also to underlining their long-term intent.

Given the explosion in international limited overs cricket and the appeal that the game holds for television broadcasters and, by extension, potential sponsors, it should surprise no-one where Irish ambitions lie. They are utterly pragmatic about the future.

Walsh explains: "We want one-day international status. That does not mean we want to enter the World Cup as of right but it would mean we could be invited to take part in one-day triangular tournaments against senior Test-playing nations."

It seems to have taken long enough for the Irish to get around to doing it. After all, it was they who staged the first international back in 1855, Ireland against eleven 'Gentlemen of

Mike Hendrick, the first full-time Irish cricket coach, in his playing days

England', 22 years before the inaugural Ashes Test between England and Australia in Melbourne.

Somehow though the game has never taken off, never gripped the nation. Not surprisingly it flourished originally in the garrison towns in the early 19th century and also in the squirearchy, where country house cricket thrived among the landed gentry with seats in Ireland.

But after partition and the founding of the Republic as an independent state in 1921, the formation of the Gaelic Athletic Association (GAA) ensured that cricket remained a minor sport south of the border. The GAA was set up as the guardian of the native sports of hurling and Gaelic football. Anyone playing these could not ay any of the so-called foreign sports of soccer, gby or cricket.

These days the Irish Cricket Union, mprising Leinster, Munster and the Northern ricket Union (Belfast) and the North West nion (Londonderry), has shown its commitment appointing Hendrick. And his commitment is ear when he states: "It's criminal that we are not there with Bangladesh and Kenya now. There certainly no reason why we can't go as far as they ve and be accorded one-day international status."

> **There is certainly no reason why we can't be accorded one-day international status.**

The disappointment at not having qualified r this year's World Cup is being countered by a ositive approach to the ICC Trophy tournament vo years hence in Canada. Success in Toronto in 01 would lead to qualification for the next orld Cup tournament in 2003.

And, as far as Hendrick (and indeed the rest f the ICU) is concerned, that is a priority. "I am en to take the side to Toronto," explains endrick, whose contract ends this December, ecause I believe Ireland can qualify for the next orld Cup."

But Hendrick and the ICU have a major stumbling block – finance. The ICU intends appointing a full-time chief executive later this year. "He is likely to be someone who knows about the big world of marketing," explains Walsh. "It is going to take a professional person to go out and get sponsorship money."

And if enough money were raised Hendrick would hope it could be used to turn his senior squad into part-time professionals. "We need to get the nucleus of our better talented boys on to semi-professional contracts - that would make a lot of difference."

Unfortunately, as Hendrick is only too well aware, that takes money and in the vicious circle that keeps all sport in a spin, to get money you need success, but to get success you need money.

The Irish have no problem competing at Under 13, Under 15 and Under 17 level, but after that the going gets tough. "If there were a financial incentive to make it attractive to the 18 and 19-year-olds, it would make a big difference," admits Hendrick.

"Rugby is professional now and where our players have dual sports and the seasons overlap, they generally go for rugby." Perhaps today's World Cup tie at picturesque Clontarf will kick start interest in the sport among the business population. •

The Irish Cricket team celebrate beating Middlesex in the 1997 Bensons & Hedges Cup

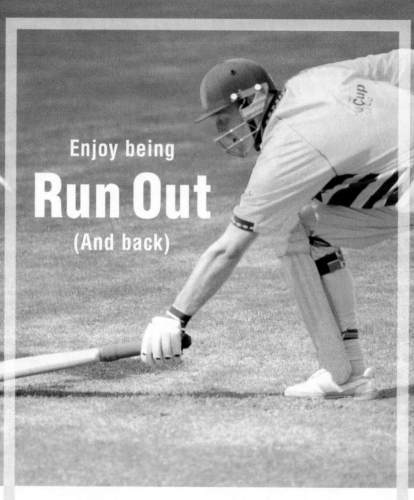

Enjoy being
Run Out
(And back)

Emirates' hospitality ensures there's never a dull moment during your flight.
There's our award-winning food and wine to savour. And your own personal in-flight
entertainment system, featuring up to 17 video and 22 audio channels.
You'd have to go out and back a few times to work your way through that little lot.

OFFICIAL SPONSOR OF THE 1999 CRICKET WORLD CUP

The tearaway with Anglo ambitions

John Blain, still only 20, will spearhead Scotland's bowling attack (and hopes to further his ambition to one day play for England). Andrew Radd met him recently.

John Blain's accent has left many shopkeepers around Northamptonshire labouring under the misapprehension that he hails from his adopted county's very own 'Little Scotland', the Celticized steel town of Corby.

The 20-year-old Edinburgh-born fast bowler may, conceivably, suffer a mild Anglo-Scottish identity crisis at some point in the future should Test cricket claim him, but for now his loyalties are anything but divided. World Cup success for his native land is top of the Blain agenda for 1999.

"Given the chance to play for my country in this tournament I obviously wasn't going to turn it down" he says. "But I've spoken to Jim Love (the former Yorkshire batsman and Scotland's coach) and he understands that I may not devote myself to Scotland in the longer term."

"I would love to play in Tests for England – no doubt about that at all. My grandmother is English, I've had a chat with my parents about it and they know what I want to do. But at the moment I've got the opportunity to represent Scotland on the biggest stage in world cricket, and that's a terrific challenge."

His emergence represents a quiet but satisfying triumph for cricket over that most omnipotent and demanding of sporting deities, soccer. Growing up in a country whose school

The Scotland team

playgrounds are littered with rather more would-be Ally McCoists, and even Gary Armstrongs, than Mike Dennesses, young Blain had his childhood sights set on World Cup glory of a different kind – until the civilised summer game replaced the winter rough-and-tumble in his affections.

> *Cricket developed into my main game. It just crept up on me and gripped me!*

"The cricket ground at Penicuik was just through the back fence of our home so I had a bat and ball in my hand from very early on, although it was always my second sport. I didn't think about it as a career because my intention was to become a footballer, and I signed schoolboy forms with Hibernian and Falkirk.

"But suddenly cricket developed into my main game, and I started to enjoy it more than soccer. It just crept up on me and gripped me!"

Blain became Scotland's youngest international cricketer in 1996, making his first-class debut against Ireland in August of that year, aged 17 years and eight months. The start of the following season found him on the professional staff at Northampton, thanks in part to the long-standing friendship between Love and one of his old colleagues from Headingley days, Northamptonshire's chief executive Steve Coverdale.

"I knew through Jim that John had been pinpointed for some time as a talented player," explains Coverdale. "He's a sportsman through and through, he knows all about the sporting environment and is a very mature individual.

"Last summer he had a knee injury which held him back, but his five wickets against Derbyshire (5-24, his victims including Dominic Cork and Phil DeFreitas) on his Sunday League debut at the back end of the previous summer showed us what he's capable of."

Thus the teenager joined the county which gave two other Scots, Alastair Storie and Jim Govan, a taste of Championship cricket not so long ago, and also brought through the towering Inverness-born paceman David Larter, who made ten Test appearances for England in the 1960s.

Blain's own international horizons were broadened considerably and memorably in the spring of 1997 when, as a member of Scotland's

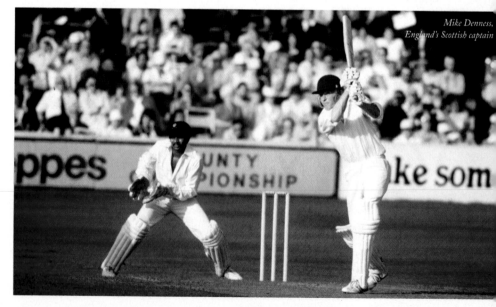

Mike Denness, England's Scottish captain

John Blain

on home soil. That showing, combined with a NatWest Trophy victory over Worcestershire in Edinburgh, gave morale a timely boost. It was a different story, predictably, against a powerful and experienced Australia 'A' team, although Blain believes it essential that the Scots are tested regularly by opponents of that calibre if standards are to improve.

"We're a bit naïve in terms of world cricket, and we need quality players to visit Scotland so we can learn from them. Allan Border came with the Australians last year and at the end of the tour he took time out to do a question-and-answer session, which gave our guys a chance to find out how the Test nations approach things.

"I think we are slowly getting some respect from the Scottish public. We grabbed a few headlines when we qualified for the World Cup, and people now realise that cricket is played here, but we're always up against soccer and rugby. Hopefully, through this tournament, we'll

> *Hopefully, we'll gain more credibility and recognition from our own population and in the rest of the world.*

gain more credibility and recognition from our own population and in the rest of the world."

This personable, articulate and ambitious young Scot is aiming high, for 1999 and beyond. He negotiated the fence between his back garden and the cricket field at Penicuik safely enough; now other even more daunting obstacles await his attention. But, as the guru Border teaches his disciples, 'Nothing worthwhile in life comes easily.'

Don't be surprised if the fame of John Angus Rae Blain spreads a good deal further south than Berwick-upon-Tweed in the years to come. Even as far, perhaps, as Corby.   •

Andrew Radd writes and broadcasts on cricket from the heart of his beloved Northamptonshire

CC Trophy squad, he flew to Malaysia with the m of helping his country secure a World Cup ot for the first time. Four victories in the group ages – Blain picking up three cheap wickets in e win over Hong Kong – sent George Salmond's en into the quarter-finals. The rain fell, but a ucial success against Denmark meant the last ur; and then the bubble burst as Bangladesh flicted a 72-run defeat in the semi-finals.

So everything hinged on the third-place lay-off meeting with Ireland at the Tenaga ports Ground. Another soggy two-day ncounter, watched by Blain from the non-ombatant side of the boundary rope, ended in iumph – and convinced at least one young ricketer of the value of thorough preparation.

"It was a great experience for me," said Blain. We worked hard on acclimatising, and to go out here and play as well as we did was a real chievement. The conditions were so different – nd when it rains, believe me, it rains! Just wenty minutes' worth can wash out a game."

Scotland turned the tables on Bangladesh in 998, comfortably winning two one-day matches

WARNING
This CD contains language
which some people may find
offensive

The 12th Man
IT'S JUST NOT CRICKET (volumes 1 & 2)

n is **AUSTRALIA'S LEGENDARY, MILLION-SELL**
is outrageous recordings are **OFF-THE-WALL**
E SEND-UPS of cricket, and more particularly, t
led by **RICHIE BENAUD, TONY GREIG, BILL LA**
w, at last, **THE 12TH MAN**, the mad Aussie so
ve heard about, but not actually heard, is **AVA**
h Man's silliest moments are on a **SPECIALLY P**
itled "IT'S JUST NOT CRICKET" (Vols. 1 & 2)

Specially Priced Double CD Set
"IT'S JUST NOT CRICKET"

thman.com   (Vols. 1 & 2)

A whole new ball game

by Jim Holden

[Am]inul Islam, one-time promising [pr]ofessional footballer and now captain [of] World Cup newcomers Bangladesh, [pr]epares to do a nation proud.

Cricket's World Cup is a unique chance for the game to show off its excitement and entertainment value in [a] modern sporting world that seems [in]creasingly obsessed with football.

Many potential cricketers in modern times [ha]ve been lost to the fabulous millionaire riches [of] the rival ball game, with Manchester United [br]others Phil and Gary Neville being classic [ex]amples.

Maybe even two of the most famous [pla]yers of all time, Sir Garfield Sobers and Viv [Ri]chards, might have chosen soccer as their [ma]in sport if the rewards had been greater [wh]en they started.

Both Sobers and Richards played [int]ernational football, for Barbados and Antigua [res]pectively. And the same would certainly have [be]en true of Bangladesh's World Cup skipper, [M]ohammad Aminul Islam Bulbul, if he had [no]t suffered a knee injury that curtailed a [hu]gely promising soccer career at the age of 19.

It forced the engaging Aminul, as he is [mo]st frequently known, to turn to his other [pas]sion of cricket to fulfil his sporting dreams.

And how they are being fulfilled as [Ba]ngladesh proudly take the World Cup stage [for] the first time in their history, hoping to [pro]ve they are worthy of Test match status.

"Of course it is the greatest moment in the [his]tory of our cricket," says the 31-year-old [rig]ht-hand bat and part-time off-spinner. "It [wa]s a wonderful feeling to win the ICC Trophy [wh]ich ensured we qualified, but playing against

Aminul Islam

Gordon Greenidge

the big nations like Australia, West Indies, New Zealand and Pakistan is so special. It is the highlight of my career for sure.

"This is the best tournament in the world. We want to play as well as we can. It is great exposure for us."

Bangladesh, who enjoy fanatical support at home, are also benefitting from the presence of the great former West Indies opener, Gordon Greenidge, as coach.

"Gordon has been with us for about two and a half years," said Aminul. "He has been so helpful, sharing his experience, teaching us good techniques. He was a truly great player and he is still a wonderful personality.

"When Gordon came we weren't playing too well. We were having a bad time. We had never qualified for the World Cup. His first assignment was to win the ICC Trophy in Malaysia and we did that.

"Since then we have beaten West Indies A when they visited Dhaka. We have been improving game by game since he arrived.

"That is why it was such good experience to play England's one-day side in a friendly match when they came for the mini-World Cup held in Dhaka last October.

"I scored 60 not out against the English bowlers then, and I also scored 121 playing against the England A side when they came to Bangladesh a few years ago. I seem to quite like the English!"

> ❛ *The softly-spoken skipper has been the heartbeat of the side.* ❜

Those innings proved what his countrymen know, that he is not only the best batsman in Bangladesh, but also a cricketer who can do well on the world stage. After making his international debut in the Asia Cup against India in 1989, the softly-spoken skipper has been the heartbeat of the side, averaging in the mid-thirties with the bat.

Aminul does have previous personal experience of cricket in England. He played two seasons for Birstall CC in the Central Yorkshire League, as well as a season at the Ringwood club in Melbourne.

Shahriar Hossain, Banglades

At home he plays for the Biman club,
ch won the Bangladeshi Premier League
npionship in January this year. Aminul led
the front with a batting average of 49.27.
He strongly feels that Bangladesh should
granted the Test status they are currently
ing from the ICC. It is the only way, he
, that further development can take place.
'Maybe we are not that experienced as

Shafiuddin Ahmed

> *We are hoping the ICC will grant*
> *Test status to Bangladesh soon.* **'**

rnational cricketers," explains Aminul. "But
hink everything is in place. We do have a
derful national stadium, which all the other
s who played in the tournament last year
ed was a great cricket ground. They also
ed the final of the Asian Test championship
veen Pakistan and Sri Lanka there.
"We are hoping the ICC will grant Test
us to Bangladesh soon. We are improving the
ities and the structure of our cricket. It is the
ber one sport in the country at the moment.
"What we have to do is play well in the
rld Cup to prove our case. But personally I
eve we should become a Test country. As Sri
ka and Zimbabwe have shown, it is the way
ally help the sport grow in a country."
What a sport also needs is great heroes and
t deeds. If anyone can do that for Bangladesh
his World Cup it is Aminul, whose
version from soccer to cricket is now total.
He adds: "I was a soccer player to begin
, playing the first division of our national
ue for three years from the age of 16 to 19. I
played in the soccer Youth World Cup in
tralia. But then I had the knee injury and
to stop.
"But I had always played schools cricket, and
s also playing first division cricket at the age
4. My first scoring shot was a sixer, I remember!
once the football ended I became very serious
ut my cricket. Now cricket has my heart." •

Holden writes on cricket and soccer for The Express.

'Was' on the warpath

When Pakistan won the World Cup in 1992, Imran Khan asked his players to "fight like cornered tigers". Now he profiles the biggest tiger of them all, Wasim Akram.

Wasim Akram

Wasim Akram originally won a place in Pakistan's Test team by actually achieving what most schoolboys can only fantasise about.

I can recall when he was one of a group of club bowlers invited to bowl at a net session for the Test squad selected to tour New Zealand in 1984. But, to everyone's amazement, the 18-year old unknown from Lahore proved to be far more awkward for the batsmen than those pacemen already chosen.

So, he was immediately added to the touring team and, in only his second Test in New Zealand, picked up 10 wickets in the match!

Thus started the amazing career of Wasim Akram, who along with Michael Holding was the most naturally talented fast bowler of my time. Bear in mind, that the past 20 years have seen the greatest number of fast bowlers in the history of cricket.

Wasim has been blessed with a whippy side-on action, with which he can still generate tremendous pace off the pitch. However, it is his powerful wrist action which has enabled him to seam and swing the ball both ways at pace which has made him lethal.

It took him a couple of years to perfect a yorker, and his dangerous bouncer, but by the end of the 1980's he had established himself as one of the most feared bowlers in world cricket.

He is already the highest wicket-taker in the history of one-day cricket - and if he can maintain his fitness nothing can stop him from breaking the Test wicket record too.

As a batsman, though, Wasim has not done

im Akram

tice to his talent, and anyone who witnessed
incredible innings of 123 at Adelaide in 1990
uld be surprised at his poor overall batting
ord. At the same time, it must be added that
has played quite a number of useful innings
Pakistan in both Test and one-day arenas.

I have always felt that Wasim is ideally suited
lead Pakistan, as he has most of the qualities
eded to captain a cricket team. Firstly, he has
vays been a team man and never a selfish
cketer; secondly he has always been popular
thin the team, and has time to sit and talk to
eryone; and, most significantly, he is an
-rounder.

My belief is that all-rounders often make the
st captains as they naturally look at the game
m both a batsman and bowler's point of view.
me of the best captains of my time were
-rounders: Mike Procter, Clive Rice and Tony
reig, for instance. Pakistan's best captain was
afeez Kardar, an all-rounder, and Richie
naud is considered by most to be Australia's
st ever captain. Benaud himself, though, once
d me the best captain of his own time was
ith Miller.

So, once I retired from cricket in 1992, I
commended Wasim as the most logical choice
my successor as Pakistan captain. Unfortunately
Wasim, his first series was against the West
dies in the Caribbean. And, although he was
pected to make some mistakes in his first series
leader, and hopefully learn from them, there
s a players' rebellion against him several
onths after that series.

I believe that a big turning point in
Pakistan's recent cricket history happened then.
The Pakistan Cricket Board rewarded the
players' conspiracy by removing Wasim from the
captaincy. But, if they had stood firm and backed
Wasim, I believe the Pakistan team would have
dominated the world of cricket for the past five
or six years. Pakistan possessed the best fast
bowlers and the best spinners in international
cricket and was poised to take over the top slot
from the West Indies.

Instead, the PCB made a fatal mistake and
Wasim's removal from the captaincy at that time
completely destabilised Pakistan's most talented
Test team. Between 1992 and 1999 around ten
changes were made to the team's captaincy -
including, eventually, a second term of office for
Wasim.

> **My belief is that all-rounders make the best captains.**

He then began to grow in the leadership role
and in late 1997 the West Indies were
whitewashed in a three-Test series in Pakistan.
But, upon losing a one-day tournament in
Sharjah a few weeks later, Wasim was removed
again - the official reason for this bizarre move
being his fitness.

After a few more captaincy changes he has,
at last, been brought back once more, and I feel
captaining the team at this World Cup is going
to be Wasim's most crucial role for Pakistan cricket.

Not only will his vast experience - especially
of English conditions - be important in coping
with the pressure that builds up during World
Cup matches, but also he will provide the much-
needed stability to a highly-talented team. I just
hope he has been given enough time to prepare
his players for the demands of a World Cup.

*Imran Khan crowned a regal career as one of the
world's greatest all-rounders by leading Pakistan to
World Cup glory in 1992. In 88 Tests for Pakistan
this proud man took 362 wickets at 22.81, and also
scored 3,807 runs at an average of 37.69.*

Scotland does it for Love

Bill Lothian describes how the former Yorkshire batsman will help George Salmond to leap into public recognition.

For Scottish cricket the great adventure is only just beginning. Regardless of how the team fare in their first sortie into the finals of the World Cup - and on grounds of effort alone skipper George Salmond's men will undoubtedly not be found wanting - many more exciting opportunities loom on the horizon, according to Jim Love, the Scottish Cricket Union's director of cricket.

Pride of place among these projects undoubtedly goes to the new National Indoor Cricket Centre, due to come on stream next year in Edinburgh though, by then, the game in Scotland could also be enjoying the benefits of three other schemes that can surely only mean a higher profile north of the border.

This summer saw the first truly National League established in a ploy calculated to intensify competition among the top home-based players.

Also, moves are afoot which could see Scotland rewarded with one-day international

Jim Love playing for Yorkshire

status - a stepping stone to raising standards through, at the very least, the likely requirement to provide a number of first-class domestic fixtures.

And, of course, it is now accepted in Scottish cricket's corridors of power that the national side must have its own easily identifiable ground.

As Scotland went into World Cup action, however, it was the new Indoor Centre, due to be

> ❛ *Scotland's representatives did so well to come through, qualifying with minimal help up until now.* ❜

officially opened next June, which offered the most visible sign of Scottish cricket's rapid development.

Love said: "I've got what I wanted at last - a dream come true in the form of a facility I have been screaming for during most of the past five years.

"What is particularly appealing about the Centre is the fact that, at long last, Scottish cricketers will soon be operating on proper run-ups and with video analysis to aid their development.

"Really, it should never be forgotten that, in reaching the World Cup finals, Scotland's representatives did so well to come through, qualifying with minimal help up until now."

It perhaps puts that situation into perspective to recall how former England fast bowler Graham Dilley came to be invited on board as a lieutenant to Love for the great World Cup crusade.

Love was invited to Trent Bridge, Nottingham, by former Yorkshire colleague Martyn Moxon, in the hope that there might be benefits for him and Scotland from watching the England A side preparing for last winter's tour of Zimbabwe and South Africa.

The former England one-day batsman said: "When I arrived at the ground I immediately became aware that the England A players had the assistance of no fewer than seven specialist coaches plus managerial and medical back-up.

...ham Dilley playing for England in 1989

himself to be in charge at all times on the field.

"Woe betide the bowler who chances his arm in trying to insist on another over when it is clear he is not producing.

"There is an inner steel about George which contrasts with his laid-back attitude at other times."

By the time the new Indoor Centre is hopefully churning out the George Salmonds of the future, Scottish cricket should also have identified its equivalent to football's Hampden Park or rugby's Murrayfield Stadium.

Love said: "Of course, there will still be a need for the Scotland team to continue playing games around the country. But that shouldn't take away the need for a base where we can produce pitches that we want to play on, rather than continually having to operate on club-type pitches."

> **❛** *George has done such a good job without quite managing to shed his image as the joker of the team.* **❜**

"Back in Scotland I invariably found myself ...empting to do all those tasks myself and, while ..t was a challenge I relished, a bit of assistance, ...ecially in the bowling department was never ...ng to go amiss."

Wheels were set in motion to increase the ...ertise available to the Scottish players and, with ...ley agreeing to take up an offer to help, a final ...ce in the jigsaw fell into place.

Without the element of credibility attained by ...otland through their heroics in qualifying for the ...orld Cup finals out in the steamy heat of Kuala ...mpur, it is debatable how much funding would ...ve been available for the type of planning ...eded to ensure that a legacy remains from the ...m's relative success so far.

But what a legacy it now promises to be for a ...m currently led energetically by Salmond. Love ...ded: "George has done such a good job without ...ite managing to shed his image as the joker of ...e team.

"Inevitably it is George who is behind those ...ssing boot-laces or early morning phone-calls, ...t when it is time to be serious he has always ...own exactly what was required.

"Every decision is made objectively and George ...s done very well tactically besides showing

Scotland's aim, in short, is that some of the first players to walk through the doors of the new Centre will be the ones with the responsibility to ensure that qualifying for World Cup finals is soon regarded as the norm in Scottish cricket.

But why stop there, and what are the prospects for, say, a Test series involving Scotland?

John Everett, chairman of the Scottish Cricket Union, is bullish about the prospect, predicting "20 years" when asked to put a date on when that great day might dawn.

Before then there is much work to be done but Everett is convinced that one-day international status would be a significant carrot.

He said: "One-day international status for Scottish cricket could be a huge boost if it comes at the right time.

"I'm convinced that continued success out in the middle can only strengthen Scottish cricket's hand when it comes to the pursuit of the funding which we need to take the game forward." •

Bill Lothian is a sportswriter with the Edinburgh Evening News.

Children's competition fun page

World Cup England 99

Have some fun trying out the following puzzles and quiz.

Test your knowledge and word power against your friends.

Can you find all the word in the grid?

How good is your cricket knowledge?

Hidden here are 10 cricketing words: can you find them?

The words are:

BOWLER, GULLY, BACKWARD SHORT LEG, SQUARE LEG, EXTRA COVER, LONG ON, THIRD MAN, STUMPED, RUN OUT, WIDE

CRICKET ANAGRAMS

ZWTOHA
UCONRBE
LIPVINAO
NSGITCEHRSE
IANRTEEDL
YRBNAUDO
NNGWAAHTTIHMC
PEEONR
TANMASB
MUOTANTRE

```
B A K N Z N L A W C L D Q S V E T F P S
L O H F I A B K B C I Q G K K G H E R C
Q X W B V J A A C E J B Q F O C D P J Z
S G E L T R O H S D R A W K C A B U P P
G M K R E U F T U R X U H E G U L L Y C
B D K D N R A S G N Q D A B C P E O W X
L R V M T V Q P P P O O I S O E T L M L
Z U C R X Z I R U N O U T J T T K V V S
B X H W S S R O F O D D Z G J H K D M I
U W I D E T L N A H R D C I N I Z O W X
J V Q V T H N B G R E M X J M R L Y U R
V X X M W W C E I X V F L F Y D K F U E
P Z N X K X L O N G O N O Z P M Q A T L
Y R A H D E X L X Q C G E D Q A K U C J
P V B B R C W Z E D A P F J E N E X T H
H A O U F Z W X P R R S Q S R P S J N D
C G A C C R D E B D T P K S E L M K H I
S Q C K D Z O O I F X J Z I W V N U G C
S A O D G N Y S M H E G H M M L B N T J
M A N U X N E W L T W A X Y T I V F P S
```

QUIZ (Adults - please keep away!)

1. Who captained England in the first World Cup?
2. How many different teams have competed in the World Cup (including this one!)?
3. How many different countries have won the World Cup?
4. Who has played in the most one-day internationals?
5. Who holds the record for the fastest one-day international hundred?
6. At what other sport has Jonty Rhodes represented South Africa?
7. Who scored the most runs at the 1996 World Cup?
8. Who has hit the highest individual score in World Cup competition?
9. How many one-day internationals did Sir Garry Sobers play in?
10. Who is the oldest century-maker in one-day international history?

lowers in full bloom
or Zimbabwe

**rk Williams looks at Zimbabwe's
during cricketing dynasties.**

R arely, if ever, has a country been so well
served by cricketing families as
Zimbabwe is today. Streaks, Whittals,
angs, Matambanadzos, Rennies and Flowers -
name them all is to wonder if there is any
nbabwean family that has been left out!

If Heath Streak, Zimbabwe's main strike
vler, and his father, Dennis, are an unusual
nbination, Dennis being a national selector
l former first-class cricketer, the remaining
nilies boast two current first-class cricketers
o, with one exception, have all played Test
l one-day international cricket. The Whittall
isins, Guy and Andrew, and the Strang
others, Paul and Bryan, comprise a balanced
vling attack in themselves - to say nothing of
iy Whittall's prowess with the bat.

And while the Matambanadzo brothers
ght suffer in comparison since all-rounder
rlington, the elder twin, has not so far played
international level, their best days may well lie
the future. Fast bowler Everton
atambanadzo's Test career was interrupted last
ar by a shin injury. This saw him sidelined for
ost of a season in which Henry Olonga and
m Mbangwa were busy cementing their places
Zimbabwe's Test attack.

Last season too witnessed Gavin, the
unger of the Rennie brothers, come of age as a
est batsman. His cultured 84 in the second
nings against India at Harare in October was
strumental in setting a fourth innings target
hich ultimately proved too much for India's
ar-studded batting line-up. Brother John,
eanwhile, has taken something of a back seat
nce the 1996-97 Tri-Nation series against India
d South Africa when his outstanding swing

Andy Flower (above)   *Grant Flower (below)*

Paul Strang

bowling featured in a number of impressive performances by Zimbabwe.

But, pride of place in Zimbabwe's family affair must go to the Flowers, sons Andy and Grant and their father, Bill. While John Rennie, Bryan Strang and Everton Matambanadzo have to be content with being on the reserve list for the World Cup, no such fate was ever likely to befall Zimbabwe's current premier cricket family. Andy and Grant Flower are key members of the World Cup party, while back home their father, Bill, is playing a vital role in promoting cricket in Zimbabwe's majority black community.

Indeed, the Flower contribution to cricket development in Zimbabwe is something of which they can be justifiably proud. Having taught his young sons the fundamentals of the game and launched them on the road to stardom, Bill was not content to sit back and admire their performances. A fine cricketer himself in his youth, he moved on from coaching Andy and Grant to being both an administrator and coach at schoolboy level.

But Bill's greatest contributions have come in recent seasons. These have seen his focus moving from Harare's genteel northern suburbs to the High Density areas (former Townships) on the south side of the city. Here, he has been instrumental in helping disadvantaged youngsters pick up the rudiments of the game, as well as in assisting the emergence of the Old Winstonians as the first High Density-based club with aspirations at the national level.

Whether father took the lead from son, or vice versa, Bill's example in the High Density is mirrored by that of his elder son, Andy. It might be thought that as Zimbabwe's premier batsman and wicket-keeper, Andy Flower had enough on his plate. Certainly his voluntary relinquishing of the captaincy of the national side in 1996 suggested so. But prior to the 1998/99 domestic season he assumed the captaincy of Old Winstonians with direct responsibility not only for spearheading their campaign to climb up the League tables, but also for promoting the club and thereby the game among the masses.

> *Hard-headed realism is the principal driving force behind the success of all three Flowers on and off the field.*

Lest such commitment might be thought to be born only from idealistic motives, let there be no doubt that hard-headed realism is the principal driving force behind the successes of all three Flowers on and off the field. Andy, above all, knows that the comparative success which Zimbabwe has enjoyed at international level since its baptism in 1992/93 cannot be sustained if its cricket fraternity remains largely limited to the dwindling white community. Only by putting down substantial roots in the majority community can Zimbabwe cricket hope to have a viable international future.

Meanwhile, the two younger Flowers can look forward to further success in Zimbabwe's cause on the field. Both are now mature Test batsmen with five Test centuries each to their names. They also relish batting in harness; witness their 269-run partnership against

...istan in 1994/95, which was the foundation
Zimbabwe's first Test victory.

Andy vies with Alec Stewart as the world's
...mier wicket-keeper/batsman. Arguably the
...ter gloveman, his selection for the Rest of the
...rld XI against MCC last season was due
...ognition of his class. Although he had a
...ppointing World Cup on the sub-continent
1996 - a factor which prompted his giving up
...captaincy - Andy is a superb one-day
...sman, capable of fashioning unorthodox shots
...inst the best bowling. His only World Cup
...tury to date was in his first match - 115 not
...t against Sri Lanka at New Plymouth in 1992.
...t it will be no surprise if he notches up
...mber two in the present contest.

> *Andy vies with Alec Stewart
> as the world's premier
> wicket-keeper/batsman.*

In contrast, and to the surprise of those who
...tched him graft away at the crease against
...gland A in his debut season in 1989/90,
...rant Flower has now developed into a high
...ss limited-overs batsman, to say nothing of his

Guy Whittall

...ath Streak

electric fielding. Three one-day international
hundreds in 1998 underlined this advance.

Both Flowers possess sound techniques and
unflappable temperaments. Their World Cup
prospects are also enhanced by their familiarity
with English conditions. For Andy this started
with a contract when he was 19 with the Barnt
Green club in the Birmingham League.
Thereafter he enjoyed seasons with West
Bromwich Dartmouth and for Heywood in the
Central Lancashire League. In more recent
years, he has coached Epsom College and, in
1997, Oxford University. Once he had left
school, Grant followed Andy to England and has
returned each season since.

So if there is to be an early upset in the
World Cup, you could do worse by banking both
on Zimbabwe supplying it and on their success
being spearheaded by those Flowers that bloom
in the (late) spring.

*Mark Williams writes on cricket for a number of
publications, including The Cricketer. He is an
acknowledged authority on Zimbabwean cricket.*

CASTLE LAGER
PROUD TO BE ASSOCIATED WITH
THE SOUTH AFRICAN
CRICKET TEAM

IMPORTED FROM · SOUTH AFRICA

WORLD CLASS CRICKET

WORLD CLASS BEER

ngland's poor showing in the last World Cup in 1996 tends to ershadow a previously fine cord in the quadrennial urnament.

Three times beaten finalists, 1979, 1987 and 1992, ngland also reached the last ur in both 1975 and 1983. A mi-final appearance will be e very least of Alec Stewart's de's ambitions this time.

Home conditions should give England me sort of advantage, although results in e run-up to this tournament have en dispiriting. Defeats in x of their last seven arlton and United series iternationals against ustralia and Sri anka in January and ebruary, plus three losses out f four in Sharjah in April, ill not have done much for nglish confidence.

But, on closer inspection, nd if they really do have an verall game plan, England seem to ossess a well-balanced squad, well-suited o early-summer conditions, and full of both character and experience. The main failing may be the fielding, which overall looks less than electric.

Graham Thorpe's fitness continues to be of prime importance to England, although the emergence of 21-year old Andrew Flintoff as a true power-hitter at international level could be a big boost to home chances. Flintoff though is by some distance the babe of a squad which, coached for the last time by David Lloyd and managed by chairman of selectors David Graveney, could end up being dubbed either the 'Golden Oldies' or 'Dad's Army'.

Whatever happens, however, England must surely be capable of topping their 1996 performance when they were finally put out of their misery by eventual winners Sri Lanka in the quarter-finals, having beaten only Holland and the United Arab Emirates at the group stage. •

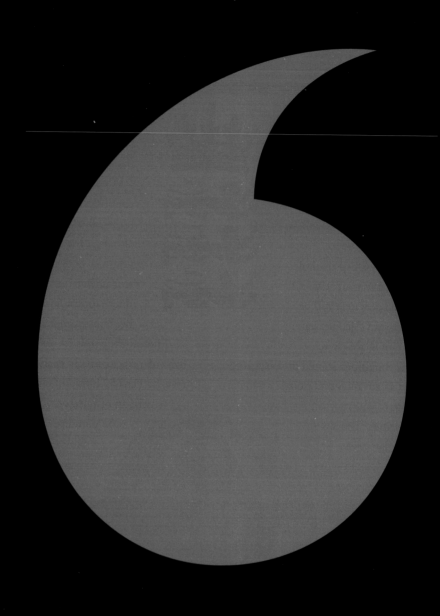

Fanatical sponsors of the 1999 Cricket World Cup.

ALEC STEWART (C)

RHB WK
Born 8 April 1963

England's captain and man for all seasons. There have been few cricketers in history capable of mastering the many different roles that Stewart has undertaken in his country's cause. Is simply indispensable in the limited-overs game where there is no argument ׀ut his role as a top order batsman and wicket-keeper. A proud ᵣrey man, and club captain, he was destined for a career in ׀fessional cricket. His father Micky also captained Surrey and ᵧed for England, besides playing football for Charlton and ׁst Ham, and was England's first manager/coach when Alec ׀ke into the Test side in 1990. In 1994 he made a century in ᵗh innings of the Barbados Test against the West Indies, and ᵗ173 against New Zealand in Auckland in 1996-97 is the ׁhest score by an England wicketkeeper.

IAN AUSTIN

LHB RM
Born 30 May 1966

This 'belt-and-braces' all-rounder, who will be 33 during this tournament, was a surprising selection as one of the Wisden's Five Cricketers of the Year. Editor Matthew Engel explained his choice with the words: "Nowadays, it is a rarity for someone to come along ᵈ establish a special rapport even with his home crowd. Ian ᵤstin is an exception. He is Lancashire to the marrow. When ᵗ succeeds, there is a special cheer in the Old Trafford pavilion ᵗcause they regard him as one of their own." Now he is one of �annland's own, too, despite non-selection for the winter Carlton ᵈ United series in Australia. First picked for a one-day ᵗernational last summer, he also went to the Wills International ᵤp in Bangladesh last autumn and is looked upon as a handy ᵃn to have around in early-summer English conditions.

ROBERT CROFT

RHB OB
Born 25 May 1970

Glamorgan's finest has now established himself as England's number one limited-overs slow bowler. Years of experience in county cricket, where he was given much responsibility at a young age, have helped to forge a crafty approach to the business of keeping batsmen quiet. His Test career, after a promising start, has lapsed somewhat, but there was never any doubt that Croft would be a key member of England's World Cup squad. A keen fisherman in his spare time, Croft is also a Welsh speaker and regards playing for England as akin to a Welsh rugby player representing the British Lions. His off-spin is based on control, changes of pace and flight, and a good arm ball. Also a solid, dependable lower-order batsman who is good enough to have opened the batting for Glamorgan in limited-overs cricket.

MARK EALHAM

RHB RM
Born 27 August 1969

Kent's chunky all-rounder is perhaps the most effective one-day cricketer in the country. He has the ability to change a game with either bat or ball, while his outfielding has the quiet brilliance of his father - the former Kent captain Alan Ealham. In 1995 he scored the fastest Sunday ᵉague century, a 44-ball effort against Derbyshire, and it was no ᵣrprise when he forced his way into England's one-day ᵢternational side the following summer. He also won the first of ᵢs eight Test caps in 1996, but it is as a one-day player that he ᵃas established himself as an England regular. Took 5-32 against ᵣi Lanka at Perth in late January and his accurate mix of swing ᵃd cut should be mightily effective in home conditions too.

NEIL FAIRBROTHER

LHB
Born 9 October 1963

One of just three survivors, alongside Alec Stewart and Graeme Hick, from the England side beaten narrowly by Pakistan in the 1992 World Cup final. An acknowledged master of pacing a one-day innings, Fairbrother's international career seemed over several years ago - especially as he suffered a succession of hamstring injuries that disrupted his Lancashire appearances. But injury to Graham Thorpe led England's selectors to recall the combative left-hander and, after playing in the Wills International Cup in Bangladesh last autumn, he underlined his worth by hitting 323 runs at an average of 64.60 in the Carlton and United series in Australia earlier this year. Made his Lancashire debut in 1982 , captained the county for two seasons in 1992-93, and has been a part of seven one-day title triumphs. Played 10 Tests between 1987 and 1993, and in 1990 hit the Surrey attack for 366 at The Oval - 311 of those runs coming in one day.

ANDREW FLINTOFF

RHB RFM
Born 2 December 1977

The cricketing boy with the power of a giant. Flintoff slimmed down from 19 stone to 17 stone last winter, starred on the England A tour of Zimbabwe and South Africa, and then forced his way into the World Cup squad on the strength of his bludgeoning batting and fast-improving seamers. Former captain of England Under 19's, and long marked out for greatness by England coach David Lloyd, Flintoff is already a favourite of the Lancashire crowd. It was at Old Trafford last season that he struck 34 off one over from Alex Tudor during a championship match. At 21 he is by far the youngest player in England's squad. Made his Test debut against South Africa at Trent Bridge last summer and showed then that he has the ability to bowl distinctly quick as well as being able to hit the ball vast distances. Made his one-day international debut during the Coca-Cola Cup in Sharjah in April.

ANGUS FRASER

RHB RFM
Born 8 August 1965

Critics will say Good Old Gus is a lucky man to be in England's World Cup squad, but the big Middlesex seamer is not the sort of character yo write off easily. Made his Test debut 1989 and was soon rated as one of th world's best bowlers. But a chronic h injury, suffered in Australia in 1990-91, threatened his whole career and f a while he had to quit cricket. Sheer determination and hard work earned him a comeback, and in early 1994 he was an England hero again with 8-75 in the historic Test win against West Indies in Barbados. In 1995 his 100th Test victim was Brian Lara but he soc found himself out of favour. Then, picked as a support act/assistant bowlers coach for the 1997-98 West Indies tour, he found himself centre stage when injury claimed Darren Gough. Fraser picked up 27 wickets in that series to equal John Snow's record for an Englan bowler in the Caribbean, and last summer followed it up with a 24 wicket haul in the series victory against South Africa. Disappointment, however, followed in Australia but he showed, on his international return in Sharjah in April, that he can still do a jol

DARREN GOUGH

RHB RF
Born 18 September 1970

England's Cornhill Player of the Year for 1998, and one of the biggest reasons for English hopes of World Cup success in 1999. Gough has been back to his ebullient best during the past 12 months, following the desperate disappointment of failing to make the previous winter's West Indies tour through injury. Problems of fitness have, in fact, dogged Gough's career to date but - when he is firing on all cylinders - there are few more potent match-winners with ball in hand than the thick-set Yorkshireman. With more luck, he could have had a decisive influence on last winter's Ashes series in Australia, and back in 1994-95 a stress fracture of the foot crippled England after Gough had taken 20 wickets in three Tests. He did, however, leave Australia with some happier memories this time - in the Fifth Test he took a hat-trick and, in the Carlton and United series which followed, he underlined his consistency and ability by snapping up 18 wickets at 27.27 runs apiece.

GRAEME HICK

RHB OB
Born 23 May 1966

England's enigma is now becoming senior citizen in one-day international terms but - 33 during this tournament - Hick remains fearsomely fit and, potentially, a fearsome opponent for any bowling attack. More effective in one-day cricket down the years - although h perceived lack of success in the Test arena is perhaps as much down to the unfairly high expectations of him as to his actual achievements. Hick remains the most prolific batsman of his generation, however, and a highly-experienced one; it is largely forgotten that he was in his native Zimbabwe's 1983 World Cup squad as a 17-year old. Scored his first 100 as a six-year old, for his school team in Harare, and in 1990 became the youngest batsman to reach 50 first-class hundreds. Last summer came his 100th first-class hundred and, at 32 years and eight days, he was but a fortnight older than the youngest man to reach that great milestone - the legendary Walter Hammond.

ADAM HOLLIOAKE

RHB RM
Born 5 September 1971

A gusty all-rounder, capable of high-class strokes and clever, innovative, medium-paced bowling. Hailed, along with younger brother Ben, as the saviours of English cricket when they both starred against Australia in the 1997 Texaco Trophy series. Adam was soon appointed as England's one-day captain, leading his side to victory in the Sharjah Cup in December 1997. But Adam endured a 4-1 reversal in the one-day series against West Indies in March-April 1998 and, although he held on to the captaincy for the 1998 Texaco Trophy series with South Africa, the appointment of Alec Stewart as Mike Atherton's Test successor meant, sooner rather than later, that the two jobs would again be combined in one man - Stewart. Born in Melbourne, of an Australian father and Balinese mother, Hollioake was schooled in England from the age of 11 and qualified for England in 1992.

NASSER HUSSAIN

RHB
Born 28 March 1968

At Test level he has been England's vice-captain since 1996, serving first under Mike Atherton and now Alec Stewart. Hussain has also cemented his place at number three with a string of big scores, but is in this World Cup squad as a late replacement for the injured Atherton, who was named in the original 15. His brilliant all-round fielding will definitely be an asset, too. Made his Test debut as long ago as 1990, in the West Indies, but injury and perceived problems of temperament combined to leave him out of international cricket for three years. A successful tour of Pakistan as captain of England A gave him a path back into the Test team, and in 1996 he returned with two centuries against India. Another hundred in Zimbabwe that winter was followed by a century and magnificent 207 against the 1997 Australians, and Hussain was back to stay.

– 48 –

NICK KNIGHT

LHB
Born 28 November 1969

Knight came of age as England's first-choice one-day opener with his brilliant innings of 122 off 130 balls, and then 90 from 107 balls, in the first two internationals against West Indies in 1998, both in Bridgetown. England lost that series 4-1, but Knight also hit a quickfire 65 in the final match in Trinidad and, despite s failure to earn a regular Test place, his name has always been the top of England's one-day batting order since he broke into e top-flight in 1996. That was the summer he scored his aiden Test hundred, against Pakistan at Headingley, and llowed it up by hitting the same bowlers for two successive e-day hundreds in the end-of-summer Texaco Trophy series. s ability to hit the ball over the top is extremely valuable in the ening 15 overs of a one-day international, but he then also has e technique and stamina to go on an play an anchor role if eded. A quite brilliant fielder, both close to the wicket and in e outfield.

ALAN MULLALLY

RHB LFM
Born 12 July 1969

Made his first-class debut as an 18-year old for Western Australia, where he was raised, and also represented the Australian Under 19 team, but he then turned down a place in the famed Adelaide Academy so as to return to Britain and seek to fulfil his ambition to play for England. Born Southend, of English-Irish stock, he was initially on ampshire's books and played one match for them in 1988. But s happy association with Leicestershire began in 1990 and so played an integral part in their championship successes of 96 and 1998. Played his first nine Tests in 1996 and early 97, but was then dropped and only came back into serious ngland contention last winter in Australia. Had a fine Ashes ries, despite being left out of the Sydney Test, and in the arlton and United series his 14 wickets came at the impressive onomy rate of exactly four runs per over.

GRAHAM THORPE

LHB
Born 1 August 1969

The England selectors have gambled on Thorpe's recovery from worryingly long-term back problems simply because he is crucial to the hopes of lifting the World Cup. The recall last winter of Neil Fairbrother was in recognition of the gaping hole left in England's middle order by Thorpe's absence. But, after flying ome last December in the middle of the Ashes campaign to rest d receive more treatment, Thorpe declared himself fit for orld Cup action and was immediately selected for the pre-urnament trip to Pakistan and Sharjah. Two half-centuries in e Sharjah tournament confirmed his return to fitness. Since 93, when he joined legends WG Grace and KS Ranjitsinhji in e elite band who have made their first Test century on debut ainst Australia, Thorpe has become one of the most respected d talented batsmen in the world. By the time he reached his th Test appearance last summer, Thorpe had made six nturies to add to his tally of 23 fifties.

England Squad One-Day Career Averages
Based on all matches played up to 30/04/1999

BATTING AND FIELDING

NAME	M	I	NO	RUNS	HS	AVGE	100	50	CT	ST
G.P.Thorpe	48	48	7	1661	89	40.51	-	16	26	-
N.H.Fairbrother	70	68	17	2035	113	39.90	1	16	33	-
N.V.Knight	44	44	3	1620	125*	39.51	3	9	15	-
G.A.Hick	91	90	9	3112	126*	38.41	5	20	45	-
A.J.Stewart	120	115	8	3253	116	30.40	2	18	104	11
A.J.Hollioake	32	29	6	600	83*	26.08	-	3	13	-
N.Hussain	28	28	5	549	93	23.86	-	2	14	-
A.Flintoff	4	4	0	85	50	21.25	-	1	-	-
V.J.Wells	9	7	0	141	39	20.14	-	-	7	-
M.A.Ealham	34	26	1	441	45	17.64	-	-	3	-
R.D.B.Croft	42	30	11	287	32	15.10	-	-	9	-
A.R.C.Fraser	39	18	8	123	38*	12.30	-	-	2	-
D.Gough	60	41	14	300	45	11.11	-	-	9	-
I.D.Austin	7	6	1	34	11*	6.80	-	-	-	-
A.D.Mullally	24	11	4	45	20	6.42	-	-	5	-

BOWLING

NAME	O	M	R	W	AVGE	BEST	5W	ECON
V.J.Wells	36.4	3	189	8	23.62	3-30	-	5.15
D.Gough	557.2	47	2388	97	24.61	5-44	2	4.28
A.Flintoff	22.2	0	132	5	26.40	2-3	-	5.91
A.R.C.Fraser	368.4	55	1301	46	28.28	4-22	-	3.52
A.J.Hollioake	183.2	4	929	31	29.96	4-23	-	5.06
A.D.Mullally	214.2	22	868	28	31.00	4-18	-	4.04
M.A.Ealham	282.2	14	1206	36	33.50	5-32	1	4.27
G.A.Hick	159.1	4	785	21	37.38	3-41	-	4.93
R.D.B.Croft	362	21	1522	40	38.05	3-51	-	4.20
G.P.Thorpe	20	1	97	2	48.50	2-15	-	4.85
I.D.Austin	60.3	1	294	3	98.00	2-37	-	4.85
N.H.Fairbrother	1	0	9	0	-	-	-	9.00

VINCE WELLS

RHB RM
Born 6 August 1965

International cricket has come late to the likeable Wells, a key member of Leicestershire's two championship triumphs in 1996 and 1998 but who, in 1991, left his native Kent after four seasons. Originally a batsman-wicketkeeper, hence his role in this squad as official understudy keeper to Alec Stewart, Wells has developed his medium pace bowling to such an extent over the years that he is now regarded as a fully-fledged all-rounder of a different sort. His flexibility could be used to the full by England in this World Cup. Made his international debut in last winter's Carlton and United series in Australia, and came of age in the first final against the Aussies, at Sydney, when he took 3-30 from his 10 overs and then scored 33 from 39 balls.

SOUTH AFRICA'S FINEST FRUIT FOR CRICKET'S FINEST TOURNAMENT.

Official Supplier to the Cricket World Cup '9

India (Group A)

The 1983 winners can never be discounted from any one-day tournament, which is their collective flair and experience of limited-overs cricket. No country plays as much of the shorter game than India - but can they produce when it really matters?

Their strength is transparently in their batting, which is itself based on the god-like talent of Sachin Tendulkar. Tendulkar's battle with Brian Lara for the unofficial title of world's best batsman could be one of the talking points of this World Cup.

India also possess three bowlers of proven world-class in Javagal Srinath, Venkatesh Prasad and Anil Kumble, but the remaining 20 overs of every opposition innings will have to be bowled by others - and that might be India's inherent weakness, along with fielding which is never the best.

As he proved in Sharjah in April, where he deputised as skipper for the injured Azharuddin, Ajay Jadeja is a sparky cricketer while Rahul Dravid may well be - in terms of pure technique - the number two batsman in the game behind the sublime Tendulkar.

India, however, have been eliminated at the group stage in three of the six previous World Cups, and last time, in 1996, departed the tournament at the semi-final stage in Calcutta where the crowd rioted at the sight of their team on just 120-8 in reply to Sri Lanka's 251. Match referee Clive Lloyd was forced to award the unfinished match to the Sri Lankans when officials failed to restart the game.

The memory of '83 is the one they will be drawing on now, and Indians everywhere still remember the euphoria of that Lord's final triumph, when Kapil Dev's side totalled only 183 but still beat the mighty West Indies by 43 runs. Mohinder Amarnath (3-12) and Madan Lal (3-31) were among the bowling heroes that day, and another player from that era, Anshuman Gaekwad, who won 40 Test caps between 1974 and 1984, is now India's coach. •

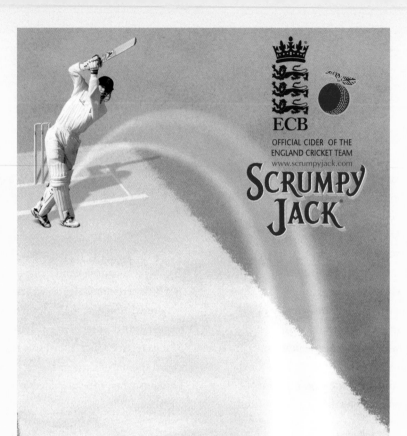

OFFICIAL CIDER OF THE
ENGLAND CRICKET TEAM
www.scrumpyjack.com

SCRUMPY JACK

don't get caught out with anything else

MOHAMMAD AZHARUDDIN (C)

RHB
Born 8 February 1963

The first player to go past 300 one-day international appearances, and at 36 is still as fit as he was in his prime. A wristy, elegant batsman and one of India's finest fielders, he now has long years of captaincy experience to draw on. Became the first cricketer to launch a Test career h hundreds in each of his first three matches, which came in 34-85 against England. Also made his one-day debut that ne winter, and in 1988 held the record for the (then) fastest ited-overs century - a 62-ball effort against New Zealand at oda. Was first made India's captain in New Zealand in 1989-celebrating with a magnificent 192 at Auckland. This is his rth World Cup campaign but, despite winning more games as ia captain than any other of his country's leaders, he has yet to ieve a major tournament triumph outside of the sub-continent Sharjah.

India Squad
World Cup

AJIT AGARKAR

RHB RFM
Born 4 December 1977

Has been rewarded with a World Cup debut for an outstanding debut season in which he reached 50 one-day international wickets faster than anyone before him. Capable of generating genuine pace from an aggressive but rhythmical run-up, Agarkar may sometimes prove ensive but the movement he gets both ways makes him an ays likely wicket-taker. Made his debut in the 1997-98 Pepsi angular tournament, against Australia - and a Test debut owed last winter, against Zimbabwe in Harare. A useful ver-order batsman, and a good fielder.

NIKHIL CHOPRA

RHB OB
Born 26 December 1973

Started out as a specialist off-spinner, but has recently developed his batting to the extent he is now regarded as an all-rounder. Has been performing consistently well in India, and is seen as the perfect support for Kumble, if required. Made his debut against Kenya at Gwalior during the 1997 Triangular tournament also involving Bangladesh. Had made 14 one-day international appearances before this World Cup, but with moderate figures. Plays for Delhi and North Zone.

RAHUL DRAVID

RHB
Born 11 January 1973

Second only to teammate Tendulkar, in terms of career average, among current Test batsmen. His 54.43 from 29 Tests is, in fact, just 0.06 of a run behind the great Sachin - evidence, if it is needed, of his class. Technically sound, he is very strong off the back foot and eschews the orthodox. If the white ball does move around significantly in s World Cup he could well be as important to India as ndulkar himself. Became the third Indian, after Sunil Gavaskar d Vijay Hazare, to score two hundreds in a Test when he hit w Zealand's attack for 190 and 103 not out at Hamilton in uary this year. Made his Test debut against England in 1996, d his one-day international bow just months earlier. Will act as reserve wicketkeeper in this squad and, almost certainly, a ure Indian captain.

SAURAV GANGULY

LHB RM
Born 8 July 1972

An effective one-day opener, and a gifted batsman too at Test level in any top-order position. Ganguly was the real find of the 1996 tour of England, hitting a superb 131 on his Test debut at Lord's on that trip. A high-born Bengali, from Calcutta, he is capable of tearing any attack apart with his wide range of strokes and his willingness to take risks. Currently ranked number six batsman in the world, with an average of 49.68 from his 27 Tests, he is also a more-than-useful seam bowler who once took 5-16 in a limited-overs international.

AJAY JADEJA
RHB RM
Born 1 February 1971

Shares with Kapil Dev the same home town of Haryana, in northern India, and in many ways is the same sort of inspirational cricketer as the former great all-rounder. Impressed with his captaincy in the recent Coca-Cola Cup tournament in Sharjah, and is a bubbly character on and off the field. His temperament, too, seems more suited to the one-day rather than the Test match stage, and he has huge experience of limited-overs internationals since making his debut against Sri Lanka in the 1992 World Cup. His first Test soon followed, but it is in one-day cricket that he is of most value to India. A flexible batsman and, on occasions, a bowler of niggling little seamers. Vice-captain.

AMAY KHURASIA
LHB
Born 18 May 1972

A heavy run-scorer in Indian cricket although he failed to make an impression when tried as a one-day opener in the recent Sharjah tournament also involving Pakistan and England. First came to be noticed when scoring a belligerent half-century for India under 25's against Graham Gooch's England at Cuttack in early 1993. Represented India at the 1998 Commonwealth Games and made his one-day international debut against Sri Lanka at Pune last winter, scoring 57. Plays for Madhya Pradesh and Central Zone.

ANIL KUMBLE
RHB LB
Born 17 October 1970

Assured himself immortality in February when he became only the second bowler in history, after Jim Laker, to take all ten wickets in a Test innings. He achieved the feat against Pakistan in Delhi and his 10-74 took his Test wicket tally to 234 in 51 matches. That overall record is also proof of his stature as one of the best leg-spinners of all time, with a style that is equally-effective in both the one-day and five-day game. Made his Test debut in England in 1990, as a 19-year old, a few months after his first one-day international appearance against Sri Lanka in Sharjah. Reached his first 100 Test wickets two matches faster than Shane Warne, and in 1995 took more than 100 first-class wickets for Northamptonshire, becoming the first leg-spinner to reach that landmark in a county season for 24 years.Great team man, a graduate in mechanical engineering, and a handy late-order hitter.

DEBASHISH MOHANTY
RHB RFM
Born 20 July 1976

One of the most promising Indian seamers to emerge for some time, and moves the ball consistently despite an unusual action. Should enjoy English conditions. Made an impressive Test debut against Sri Lanka at Colombo in 1997, including De Silva and Jayasuriya in a four-wicket haul. On that occasion he became the first player from the coastal state of Orissa to appear in a Test. Came into the World Cup with 20 wickets from 20 one-day internationals though at a cost of almost five and a half runs per over. A surprise selection, especially as he was not in the provisional list of 19.

NAYAN MONGIA
RHB WK
Born 19 January 1969

Vociferous but largely unheralded regular member of the Indian side. Succeeded his Baroda teammate and captain Kiran More as his country's first-choice wicket-keeper, making his Test and one-day international debuts against Sri Lanka in 1993-94. Before this World Cup had chalked up 131 limited-overs international appearances, and has built up a wonderful understanding with Kumble - who is not the easiest bowler in the world to keep wicket to. A solid lower middle-order batsman, he has sometimes opened the batting in Test cricket and can be employed too as a 'pinch-hitter' in the one-day game.

VENKATESH PRASAD
RHB RFM
Born 5 August 1969

An underrated but world-class opening bowler who swings and seams the ball both ways with exemplary control. Has a particularly dangerous leg-cutter, and a good slower ball. Played his first one-day international in New Zealand in 1993-94, but had to wait until 1996 to make his Test debut, and immediately impressed in that three-Test series and was named India's international Cricketer of the Year in 1997. Went past 100 one-day appearances earlier this year and is one of the most successful graduates of Dennis Lillee's fast bowling academy in Madras. A key member of the World Cup squad, given English conditions.

SADAGOPAN RAMESH

LHB
Born 13 October 1975

India's find of the winter, a dashing left-handed opener from Madras who enjoyed a prolific start to his Test career in the Asian Championship. Often hits the ball 'on the up', but has been criticised by some leading commentators already for his unwillingness to move his t. Undoubtedly one for the future for India, but he is mpletely untested in English conditions and his inclusion in e World Cup squad is at best a calculated gamble. Scored 79 ainst Pakistan and 143 against Sri Lanka in February.

ROBIN SINGH

LHB RM
Born 14 September 1963

Could have been playing in this World Cup for the West Indies, having been born and bred in Trinidad. He went to Madras to attend university, and has stayed in India ever since. Made a Test debut against Zimbabwe in Harare last winter, but has been regarded almost clusively as a one-day specialist down the years. By a quirk of e his one-day international debut, back in 1988-89, came at rt-of-Spain in his native country. A big-hitter of renown in dia, he also bowls useful medium pace and is an accomplished lder.

India Squad One-Day Career Averages
Based on all matches played up to 30/04/1999

BATTING AND FIELDING

NAME	M	I	NO	RUNS	HS	AVGE	100	50	CT	ST
S.R.Tendulkar	211	204	20	7801	143	42.39	21	43	71	-
S.C.Ganguly	99	94	8	3511	130*	40.82	6	25	30	-
M.Azharuddin	315	290	52	8949	153*	37.60	7	56	148	-
A.D.Jadeja	164	149	29	4360	119	36.33	5	25	49	-
R.S.Dravid	80	73	5	2365	123*	34.77	3	16	35	1
R.R.Singh	80	64	15	1340	100	27.34	1	5	15	-
S.Ramesh	7	7	0	189	82	27.00	-	2	-	-
N.R.Mongia	132	88	29	1222	69	20.71	-	2	101	43
A.R.Khurasia	4	4	0	71	57	17.75	-	1	-	-
N.Chopra	14	7	1	97	39	16.16	-	-	4	-
A.B.Agarkar	36	18	3	215	30	14.33	-	-	13	-
J.Srinath	161	83	24	678	53	11.49	-	1	26	-
A.Kumble	167	79	26	531	24	10.01	-	-	62	-
D.S.Mohanty	20	5	4	9	4*	9.00	-	-	5	-
Venkatesh Prasad	111	45	21	143	19	5.95	-	-	29	-

BOWLING

NAME	O	M	R	W	AVGE	BEST	5W	ECON
A.B.Agarkar	315.5	15	1656	68	24.35	4-35	-	5.24
A.Kumble	1504.1	74	6171	224	27.54	6-12	2	4.10
J.Srinath	1400.5	99	6120	220	27.81	5-23	3	4.36
Venkatesh Prasad	928.5	56	4363	134	32.55	4-17	-	4.69
S.C.Ganguly	243.1	14	1167	32	36.46	5-16	1	4.79
D.S.Mohanty	138	6	738	20	36.90	3-15	-	5.34
M.Azharuddin	92	1	479	12	39.91	3-19	-	5.20
R.R.Singh	419.1	18	2014	46	43.78	5-22	1	4.80
N.Chopra	110	6	466	10	46.60	2-21	-	4.23
S.R.Tendulkar	744	17	3645	78	46.73	5-32	1	4.89
A.D.Jadeja	203.4	2	1067	19	56.15	3-3	-	5.23
R.S.Dravid	18	0	92	1	92.00	1-21	-	5.11

JAVAGAL SRINATH

RHB RF
Born 31 August 1969

Unquestionably one of the world's leading bowlers, he spearheads the Indian attack with great pride and heart. Is deceptively quick from a shortish run-up and at his best genuinely hostile with his big inswingers and cutters. Went into this World Cup, his third, with 220 ckets from 160 one-day international appearances, and his 141 st wickets have cost just under 30 runs apiece. Had a highly ccessful season of county cricket with Gloucestershire in 1995, cking up 87 first-class wickets. Has been troubled by injury in ent years, but now seems to be over his shoulder problems. inath is also an effective hitter in the one-day game, and watch t for him being moved up the order when India need an ection of urgency with the bat.

SACHIN TENDULKAR

RHB RM
Born 24 April 1973

The best batsman in the world, in terms of technique and application. Still only 26, he is capable of re-writing all the record books - especially in one-day internationals. He came into this World Cup with 7801 runs from 211 limited-overs international appearances - including 19 centuries. At Test level he is ranked number one, with 5177 runs from 68 matches at an average of 54.49. Tendulkar was just 16 when he became India's youngest Test player, against Pakistan in 1989-90. He was 17 when he hit his maiden Test hundred, a brilliant innings to save the game against England at Old Trafford. Became Indian captain at 23, but soon handed the job back to Azharuddin so he could concentrate on his batting. Opens the innings in limited-overs cricket, and is also a handy one-day bowler with his bewildering mixture of medium-paced spinners and cutters.

ICC Cricket
World Cup
England 99 ©1997 ECB TM

MAY 14th – JUNE 20th 1999

Official Cricket World Cup
PROGRAMMES

GROUP MATCHES	£4.00
SUPER SIX MATCHES	£5.00
FINAL	£6.00

ALL PRICES INCLUDE UK POSTAGE AND PACKAGE

All match day programmes are
available by first class post.
Complete bound presentation sets
are available at discounted rates.

Call Programme Publications
on 01372 743377
or fax on 01372 743399
or email
www.eventprogrammes.com

PROGRAMME
PUBLICATIONS

Bradford House, 39a East Street, Epsom, Surrey KT17 1BL
Tel 01372 743377 • Fax 01372 743399

**Programme Publications produce
programmes for most of the
UK's major sports events**

Kenya (Group A)

Kenyan cricket truly joined the big league when Maurice Odumbe's side trounced the West Indies by 73 runs at Pune during the 1996 World Cup. That date, February 29, may well come round only every four years - but it is still recalled almost every day by cricket lovers in the next African country demanding full Test status.

This World Cup is the stage for Kenya, now with Odumbe as vice-captain to Asif Karim, to step up their demands for Test acceptance.

They qualified for England '99 by being runners-up in the 1997 ICC Trophy, surprisingly beaten by Bangladesh in the final. Odumbe was named man of the tournament after scoring 493 runs.

In Steve Tikolo the Kenyans possess another class batsman, and both Tikolo and pace bowler Martin Suji play first-class cricket in South Africa. Watch out too for the talents of Kennedy Otieno, the wicketkeeper-batsman, and all-rounders Hitesh Modi and Tom Odoyo.

Development programmes set in motion by the Kenya Cricket Association are raising standards at home, and abroad Kenya's reputation as a growing cricket nation was enhanced last May when - soon after being granted official one-day international status alongside Bangladesh by the ICC - they defeated India by 69 runs in Gwalior during a triangular Coca-Cola Cup event.

Last year, too, saw the appointment of Alvin Kallicharran as coach. Harilal Shah, a stalwart of Kenyan cricket, manages this World Cup squad and he and Kallicharran, who played 66 Tests for the West Indies, and was a World Cup winner in 1975 and 1979, will be hoping for at least one further act of giant-killing in this tournament.

DAEWOOVALU£

100% LUXURY. 50% DEPOSIT.
0% FINANCE.

With Daewoo's 50/50 finance offer you can pay 50% now and 50% in two years time (with 0% finance) on the luxurious Leganza.

Hire Purchase Example (Leganza 2.0 SX):
On the road price £14,125
Deposit £7,026.50
Nothing to pay for 24 months.
Final payment £7,026.50
Total amount payable £14,125

Offer only available on orders made before 30th June 1999. Credit provided subject to status by Daewoo Direct Finance Ltd.

Written details on request. You must be 18 or over to app and a UK resident (excluding the Channel Islands and the Isle of Man). All Daewoo Leganzas come with the following as standard:

> 1) 3 year/60,000 mile free servicing, including all parts, labour and courtesy car.
> 2) 3 year/60,000 mile free comprehensive warranty.
> 3) 3 year Daewoo Total AA cover.
> 4) 6 year anti-corrosion warranty.
> 5) Dual Airbags. 6) ABS. 7) Power Steering.
> 8) Central Locking. 9) Air Conditioning.
> 10) Electric Sunroof. 11) Alarm.
> 12) Alloy Wheels 13) Metallic Paint.
> 14) Delivery, number plates, 12 months road tax and vehicle first registration fee.

The fixed prices for the Leganza range from £14,125 to £17,825 (prices correct at time of going to press). For more information on Daewoo, or your nearest outlet, call us free on 0800 666 222.

SAVINGS BY DEALING DIRECT? THAT'LL BE THE ✺ DAEWOO VALU

ASIF KARIM (C)

RHB SLA
Born 15 December 1963

Longest-serving member of the team, having made his debut for Kenya in 1980. An insurance executive, he is also a double international having played Davis Cup tennis for Kenya. A dependable and accurate orthodox left-arm spinner, with experience of club :ket in England, and a useful hard-hitting lower order sman. Was vice-captain at the 1996 World Cup and has wide rseas experience. Took 5-33 against Bangladesh in 1997 and a one-day international top score of 53, made against mbabwe. Learnt his cricket in Mombasa, but now plays for irobi's Jaffreys Club.

Kenya
Squad

World Cup

JOSEPH ANGARA

RHB RFM
Born 8 November 1971

Bowls at a good pace, and often surprises batsmen with the speed the ball comes through on to the bat. Is, however, very inexperienced at the top level - despite making his debut back in 1995 - with only four caps to his name going into this World Cup. Attended the South African Cricket ademy four years ago, and played against India in the 1998 ca-Cola Tri-Nations tournament. Represents the Ruaraka orts Club and is a tail end batsman.

DEEPAK CHUDASAMA

RHB
Born 20 May 1963

A dentist by profession, Chudasama is finding it more and more difficult to devote time to cricket and so this World Cup is likely to be his international swansong. He has, however, already given much to Kenyan cricket. An experienced opener, who has played in three ICC Trophy events as well as the 1996 World Cup. His highest one-day international score is 122, made against Bangladesh in 1997. In that match he and Kennedy Otieno put on 225 for the first wicket, a world record at the time. Made his Kenya debut way back in 1988.

SANDIP GUPTA

RHB
Born 7 April 1967

A hard-hitting opening batsman, who also takes on the job of reserve wicketkeeper in this squad. Gupta made his Kenya debut in 1990 and has the experience of playing in three ICC Trophy events. His highest one-day international score is just 41, however. He has toured Holland, alaysia and South Africa and represents the Nairobi mkhana club. His experience has won him his World Cup ce ahead of some younger talents.

JIMMY KAMANDE

RHB RM
Born 12 December 1978

Chosen for his medium paced outswingers and his exceptional ground fielding, Kamande could yet develop into a useful all-rounder at international level. Only 20, and the second youngest member of the squad, he was a late selection with the future in mind. Has yet to make his one-day international debut but played for Kenya against a touring MCC team earlier this year. Another who plays his club cricket for Nairobi Gymkhana.

HITESH MODI
LHB ROS
Born 13 October 1971

Watch out for his batting ability in this World Cup, because Modi has improved that side of his game markedly in the last two years. Scored a vital 28 in the historic 1996 World Cup victory against the West Indies in Pune. Came into this tournament with a highest score of 78, made against Bangladesh in 1996. His bowling is less predictable. Easily the best all-round fielder in the squad.

TOM ODOYO
RHB RFM
Born 12 May 1978

Highly-promising all-rounder who played in the 1996 World Cup as a 17-year old. Dubbed 'the African Botham', he turned 21 two days before the start of this tournament and might well come of age before the end of May. Very experienced f his age, he impressed the England tourists in early 1998 and is an exciting cricketer. Like Botham, he hits the ball straight and hard, he is strongly-built, and hits the pitch hard with his quickish seamers. At the start of this World Cup his best bowling figures were 3-25, against Pakistan and his top score the 54 he made against Zimbabwe in 1997.

MAURICE ODUMBE
RHB OB
Born 15 June 1969

Man of the match in the historic 1996 World Cup victory against the West Indies after taking 3-15 in his 10 overs of well-controlled off-spin. But it is as a steady middle-order batsman, coming in after the champion Steve Tikolo, that Odumbe is most important to Kenya. A real technician, he is also blessed with a fine temperament. His highest score in the 25 one-day internationals he had played before this World Cup was an 83 made in a victory over India in last year's Coca-Cola Tri-Nations tournament. The captain at the 1996 World Cup and 1997 ICC Trophy, he also led Kenya to victory in last year's first-ever African Championship in Namibia. Is now vice-captain to Karim.

KENNEDY OTIENO
RHB WK
Born 11 March 1972

A top-order batsman in his own right, Otieno also helps to give Kenya added depth by keeping wicket in one-day international cricket. Came into this World Cup with a batting average of 32 from 2 previous internationals and also in top form: he hit 185 for the Ruarak club in Kenya's senior knock-out final in April - the last match before the squad left for England. Has scored two one-day international centuries, against New Zealand and Zimbabwe. Also made a brave 85 against Australia in the 1996 World Cup. A competent rather than naturally-talented 'keeper.

RAVINDU SHAH
RHB RM
Born 28 August 1972

Originally a middle-order batsman, he was promoted to open when he made his one-day international debut against Bangladesh at Hyderabad during the 1997-98 Coca-Cola Tri-Nations tournament. He was an immediate success, scoring 70 against India. He arrived at this World Cup with 279 runs from eight internationals at an average of almost 35, and his promising batting is supplemented by tidy medium pace. Has played a lot of English club cricket, predominantly in Hertfordshire.

MOHAMMAD SHEIK
LHB SLA
Born 16 June 1977

Both his father and uncle captained Kenya and were leading players in previous decades - and young Mohammad looks destined to have distinguished cricket career too. An extremely promising slow left-arme with a classically high action, he ha already captured 17 one-day international wickets at just 27 runs apiece before this World Cup. His best analysis, 4-36, came against Bangladesh in the recent Triangular tournament in Dhaka. He is also a hard-hittin lower order batsman, who can improve still further. Made his debut in 1997.

MARTIN SUJI
RHB RFM
Born 2 June 1971

Kenya's best and most experienced quick bowler, having played for Transvaal in 1994. He has appeared in the last three ICC Trophy tournaments, as well as being Kenya's top bowler in the 1996 World Cup. Had best bowling figures of 4-34, against Bangladesh, at the start of s World Cup and made his debut back in 1990. Plays for the a Khan club and is a useful lower order batsman.

Kenya Squad One-Day Career Averages
Based on all matches played up to 30/04/1999

BATTING AND FIELDING

NAME	M	I	NO	RUNS	HS	AVGE	100	50	CT	ST
R.Shah	8	8	0	279	70	34.87	-	3	3	-
K.Otieno	25	24	1	745	144	32.39	2	2	9	6
S.O.Tikolo	25	23	1	688	106˙	31.27	1	5	13	-
M.O.Odumbe	25	23	2	593	83	28.23	-	5	4	-
H.S.Modi	25	21	2	533	78˙	28.05	-	4	5	-
D.Chudasama	19	18	0	432	122	24.00	1	1	3	-
A.Vadher	11	9	4	102	42˙	20.40	-	-	5	-
S.K.Gupta	7	7	0	119	41	17.00	-	-	-	-
T.Odoyo	24	21	2	275	41	14.47	-	-	6	-
A.Suji	13	11	1	143	67	14.30	-	1	6	-
Asif Karim	25	17	3	167	53	11.92	-	1	4	-
M.Suji	23	17	11	48	15	8.00	-	-	8	-
M.Sheikh	15	9	4	35	15˙	7.00	-	-	6	-
J.Angara	4	2	1	6	3˙	6.00	-	-	-	-

BOWLING

NAME	O	M	R	W	AVGE	BEST	5W	ECON
M.Sheikh	99.4	1	456	17	26.82	4-36	-	4.57
S.O.Tikolo	119.2	0	603	17	35.47	3-28	-	5.05
Asif Karim	202.5	15	844	23	36.69	5-33	1	4.16
M.O.Odumbe	152.5	9	720	19	37.89	3-14	-	4.71
T.Odoyo	159	9	797	20	39.85	3-25	-	5.01
M.Suji	171	10	795	17	46.76	4-24	-	4.64
A.Suji	61.2	4	308	5	61.60	1-16	-	5.02
J.Angara	22	1	137	2	68.50	1-19	-	6.22
H.S.Modi	2	1	14	0	-	-	-	7.00
R.Shah	7	0	57	0	-	-	-	8.14

TONY SUJI
RHB RM
Born 5 February 1976

The younger brother of Martin Suji, he is a promising all-rounder who made his international debut against Pakistan during the 1996-97 Kenya Cricket Association centenary tournament. Scored 62 when he and Tom Odoyo put on a world record 119 for the seventh wicket against mbabwe at Nairobi in October 1997. Bowls medium pace swingers, and is another young cricketer Kenya hope will prove after exposure to some of the world's best.

STEVE TIKOLO
RHB OB
Born 25 June 1971

Kenya's best-known and most accomplished cricketer - perhaps the one player in their squad who can claim to be world-class. Tikolo is a destructive batsman who has scored plenty of runs at first-class level with Border in South Africa. He made 147 from 152 balls, with three sixes d 12 fours, in the 1997 ICC Trophy final against Bangladesh. 1994 he hit 1959 runs in just 18 innings in Kenya's domestic ason, a run-glut which included a knock of 224 from only 108 lls. Is well-known in Glamorgan club cricket for his ability. wls tidy off-breaks, or seamers, and as a natural athlete is a e fielder anywhere. Made 96 against Sri Lanka during the 96 World Cup and craves recognition on the bigger stage.

ALPESH VADHER
RHB
Born 7 September 1974

A batsman ideally suited in both technique and temperament to play an anchor role in the limited-overs game. Usually appears in the middle-order and, coming into the World Cup, had a top score of 42 not out against Bangladesh in the 1997-98 President's Cup. Also performed creditably against the touring New Zealanders in 1997, and Kenya hope he is one for the future. Has a good amount of overseas experience.

South Africa (Group A)

Quite properly installed as favourites for this World Cup, the South Africans have an outstanding one-day record in recent years and an enviable line-up of world-class all-rounders.

Allan Donald still leads the bowling attack with vim and vigour, and at the top of the batting order the steadiness and consistency of Gary Kirsten is another important factor.

But it is the talent in the middle of South Africa's limited-overs line-up which lies at the heart of their prolonged success in the shorter version of the game. Jacques Kallis and Shaun Pollock could both lay claim to the title of world's best all-rounder, and backing them up are Lance Klusener and Dale Benkenstein. Skipper Hansie Cronje is not only a masterful one-day captain and batsman - his medium pacers are often a valuable asset too.

Then there is Jonty Rhodes. Perhaps the best ground fielder of all time - or at least up there with the likes of Colin Bland, Learie Constantine and Clive Lloyd - he is a phenomenon over the turf and, with his fielding skills added to his unorthodox batting, Rhodes can also claim all-rounder status.

South Africa, in fact, have come a long way since being re-admitted into world cricket in 1991 following almost 21 years of isolation. And they have played a lot of cricket, both in the Test and one-day arena. It has been as if their cricketers have relished the chance for official competition after the rejection and the rebel tours of the apartheid years.

Rushed into the 1992 World Cup, after their re-admission, South Africa almost brought off one of the most stunning of triumphs. As it was, following their rain-affected semi-final exit against England, the South Africans were welcomed home like conquering heroes anyway.

In 1996 they suffered a quarter-final defeat against West Indies, who were still smarting from their embarrassing group stage loss to Kenya, but since then have brought increased know-how and mental hardness to their naturally combative play.

Central to their overall success during the past five years has been coach Bob Woolmer, the former Kent and England all-rounder whose contract with the United Cricket Board of South Africa is up at the end of this World Cup. The South Africa squad is managed by Ghulam Rajah. •

Official Motorcycle of the '99 Cricket World Cup.

Hero Honda Motors Limited. 34 Basant Lok, Vasant Vihar, New Delhi-110 057. India. Ph: 91-11-6142451, 6144121. Fax: 91-11-6143321, 614319

HANSIE CRONJE (C)

RHB RM
Born 25 September 1969

An outstanding leader, Cronje has a remarkable 75 per cent success rate as a one-day international captain after more than 100 matches in charge. He first captained South Africa at the age of 24, deputising for the injured Kepler Wessels in Australia. He was appointed full-
e at the age of 25, back in 1994-95, and one of his chief
ts as a skipper is his ability to remain calm under pressure.
s forged a close working relationship during the past five years
h coach Bob Woolmer, and their attention to detail when
rking out the strengths and weaknesses of the opposition has
n copied by other countries. Cronje is also one of South
ica's key one-day players; a hard-hitting batsman who can be
astating against spin bowlers, be brings a sense of urgency to
crease and is an aggressive runner between the wickets. He is
a steady medium-pace bowler and athletic fielder.

South Africa Squad

World Cup

DALE BENKENSTEIN

RHB RM
Born 9 June 1974

Benkenstein opted to try for the South African team despite qualifying by birth to play for Zimbabwe. He captained South Africa at schoolboy, under 19, under 24 and A team level before being part of the winning Commonwealth Games team in 1998 and finally
ning official one-day international colours during the ICC
rnament in Bangladesh at the start of the 1998-99 season. A
oke-playing batsman and outstanding outfielder, he has shown
od temperament and made his first international half-century
help South Africa beat the West Indies at Newlands after they
d been 68 for six. Has played for Natal since the 1993-94
son, during which he impressed the England A touring team.
s a father and two brothers involved in top-class cricket, and
s experience of playing in the Lancashire League.

NICKY BOJE

LHB SLA
Born 20 March 1973

A tidy slow left-arm bowler, capable left-handed batsman and lively fielder, Boje has taken over as South Africa's number one limited overs slow bowler following the retirement of Pat Symcox. He showed his big match temperament in helping South Africa win a tense Commonwealth Games semi-final against Sri Lanka on the way to a gold medal triumph against Australia. His international breakthrough came on the South Africa A tour of Zimbabwe at the start of the 1994-95 season, during which he made his maiden first-class century. A former South Africa schools captain, he made his senior international debut in Zimbabwe in 1995-96.

MARK BOUCHER

RHB WK
Born 3 December 1976

Boucher won his first Test cap at 20 when he was flown to Pakistan as an emergency replacement for Dave Richardson in 1996-97. When Richardson retired later during the same season, Boucher stepped into his place and has performed beyond expectations, holding some acrobatic
ches and proving a capable lower order batsman. He made a
iden Test century against the West Indies but has not yet had
ny opportunities to shine in one-day internationals. His
ghest limited-overs score to date is 51, made against the West
dies in his native town of East London last winter.

DEREK CROOKES

RHB OB
Born 5 March 1969

Crookes, whose father Norman toured England with the South African team in 1965 without playing in a Test, has followed in his father's footsteps as a capable off-spin bowler. He captained SA Schools in 1988. Although his spin bowling has not developed to its full potential, he is a useful performer in one-day matches and a successful batsman, scoring quickly and consistently. Like many of his teammates he is an excellent fielder, and he gets his World Cup chance largely as a result of the decision by Pat Symcox to retire from the international stage. A stalwart of Natal.

DARYLL CULLINAN

RHB OB
Born 4 March 1967

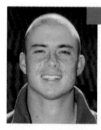

It took Cullinan several years to overcome the burden of unrealistic expectations imposed by his feats as a schoolboy prodigy, notably his achievement of scoring a first-class century at the age of 16 to succeed the great Graeme Pollock as the youngest South African player to achieve this mark. He has blossomed in recent seasons, however, and eclipsed another Pollock record with a new South African Test innings high of 275 not out against New Zealand in Auckland in 1998-99. He also holds the South African domestic record with an innings of 337 not out for Transvaal against Northern Transvaal in 1993-94. An experiment of using him as an opening batsman in one-day games has been only a partial success. Occasional off-spin bowler. His highest one-day international score, of 124, was made against Pakistan in Nairobi in 1996-97.

ALLAN DAWSON

RHB RFM
Born 27 November 1969

Brought into the squad as a late replacement for Makhaya Ntini. Dawson is a steady performer in domestic cricket, but has done we in his limited opportunities to pla internationally. First impressed th South African selectors with a gu 4-44 in sweltering conditions for A team in Sri Lanka in 1998. He then replaced an injured La Klusener in the senior South African squad at the Commonwealth Games. Put on 35 for the last wicket with Ni Boje to snatch victory against Sri Lanka in the semi-final. The South Africans, of course, finally won gold medals. Made his official one-day international debut in the mini World Cup in Bangladesh last autumn.

ALLAN DONALD

RHB RF
Born 20 October 1966

South Africa's match-winning fast bowler, he will be a key member of the World Cup side. He has taken most wickets for his country in both Tests and one-day internationals. Although widely regarded as the fastest bowler in world cricket, he seldom takes the new ball in one-day matches. Instead he usually comes on after about 12 overs when the white ball does not swing as much as at the start of an innings. Has vast knowledge of English conditions, having played regularly for Warwickshire since 1987. His home is now in Birmingham, and he has already shown a natural expertise as a bowling coach, as well as maintaining his status as one of the world's most feared pacemen.

STEVE ELWORTHY

RHB RFM
Born 23 February 1965

Choosing to concentrate on his studies for a commerce degree afte leaving school, Elworthy was a late developer as a provincial cricketer. Even so, he played first-class crick for ten years before winning international honours at the age of 33 when he was picked for the one day triangular series against Pakistan and Sri Lanka. The tall Elworthy is able to generate lively pace and is also a capable lower order batsman. He has been on two tours with the South African team, to England in 1998 and New Zealand in 1998-9 on both occasions being drafted in as a replacement for an injured player. He was man of the match in his second Test match when he took four wickets in each innings to help Sout Africa win the third and final Test and clinch the series in New Zealand.

HERSCHELLE GIBBS

RHB
Born 23 February 1974

Gibbs made his breakthrough at international level during the 1998-99 season after being switched to opening batsman in the Test series against the West Indies. Having made his first-class debut for Western Province at the age of 16, he took some time to establish his career. He had a highly successful tour of England with the South Africa A team in 1996 and made his international debut during the following season. His performances were sporadic until he made a maiden one-day international century against the West Indies and followed up by making 211 not out and 120 in successive Test matches on South Africa's tour of New Zealand. He is an exceptional outfielder, with many South African supporters believing he is the equal of Jonty Rhodes.

JACQUES KALLIS

RHB RFM
Born 16 October 1975

A highly-talented young batsman with a good technique, Kallis has established himself in the difficult number three position in both Test matches and one-day international With an unflappable technique an temperament, he was man of the series in the Test matches against t West Indies and has made Test centuries against four different countries. Strongly-built, he bowls outswingers at a lively pace and is a safe catcher in the slips or the outfield. He was man of the match in both the semi-final and final when South Africa won the 'mini World Cup' ICC tournament in Dhaka, Bangladesh, at the start of the 1998-99 season. Played for Middlesex in 1997, and will join Glamorgan at the end of the World Cup.

GARY KIRSTEN

LHB
Born 23 November 1967

A left-handed opening batsman, Kirsten is a gritty, determined player who became South Africa's all-time leading Test run-scorer during the recent series in New Zealand. He has been a prolific scorer in limited overs internationals, playing the anchor role in many high-scoring ...gs. He set a World Cup individual record when he made ...ot out against the United Arab Emirates in Rawalpindi in ...96. He was unaware that he needed only one more run to ...l Viv Richards' record for all limited-overs internationals. ...vent on to make 391 runs (average 90.30) in the tournament, ...l exceeded only by Sachin Tendulkar, Mark Waugh and ...inda de Silva. A reliable fielder, and half-brother of former ...gbok Peter Kirsten.

South Africa Squad One-Day Career Averages
Based on all matches played up to 30/04/1999

BATTING AND FIELDING

NAME	M	I	NO	RUNS	HS	AVGE	100	50	CT	ST
G.Kirsten	103	103	11	3815	188*	41.46	8	22	33	1
W.J.Cronje	159	148	27	4825	112	39.87	2	34	60	-
J.H.Kallis	64	62	10	2073	113*	39.86	5	11	27	-
L.Klusener	53	44	11	1307	103*	39.60	1	8	11	-
D.J.Cullinan	113	109	12	3413	124	35.18	3	22	50	-
J.N.Rhodes	151	137	28	3572	121	32.77	1	16	74	-
D.M.Benkenstein	10	9	3	193	69	32.16	-	1	1	-
S.M.Pollock	70	51	17	1005	75	29.55	-	4	18	-
H.H.Gibbs	27	27	1	606	125	23.30	1	1	12	-
D.N.Crookes	24	17	4	243	54	18.69	-	1	16	-
S.Elworthy	15	3	2	15	14*	15.00	-	-	4	-
N.Boje	18	8	3	74	28	14.80	-	-	6	-
M.V.Boucher	30	21	4	199	51	11.70	-	1	41	2
A.A.Donald	112	27	12	74	13	4.93	-	-	14	-
A.C.Dawson	1	0	0	0	0	0	-	-	-	-

BOWLING

NAME	O	M	R	W	AVGE	BEST	5W	ECON
A.C.Dawson	9	0	51	1	51.00	1-51	-	5.67
A.A.Donald	991	69	4012	190	21.11	6-23	2	4.04
S.M.Pollock	611.2	57	2390	103	23.20	6-35	1	3.90
D.J.Cullinan	28	0	120	5	24.00	2-30	-	4.28
S.Elworthy	100.4	8	501	20	25.05	3-21	-	4.97
L.Klusener	411.4	17	2017	73	27.63	6-49	4	4.89
J.H.Kallis	279.2	10	1339	44	30.43	5-30	1	4.79
N.Boje	132.4	5	577	17	33.94	3-33	-	4.34
W.J.Cronje	793.2	31	3448	101	34.13	5-32	1	4.34
D.N.Crookes	143.5	2	688	15	45.86	3-30	-	4.78
D.M.Benkenstein	2	0	13	0	-	-	-	6.50
G.Kirsten	5	1	23	0	-	-	-	4.60

LANCE KLUSENER

LHB RFM
Born 4 September 1971

A potential match-winner as a hard-hitting left-handed batsman and wicket-taking fast-medium bowler, Klusener has a penchant for the spectacular. He took eight for 64 against India in Calcutta in the second innings of his Test debut and made a century off 100 balls against ...ame opponents in his fourth Test match in Cape Town. He ...aken five wickets in an innings on four occasions in one-day ...national cricket and has played some major innings as a ...h-hitter including 99 in the final of the Pakistan Centenary ...drangular tournament in Lahore in 1997-98 after taking six ...ets in the round robin game between the two teams. He hit ...iden one-day international century during the recent tour of ... Zealand.

SHAUN POLLOCK

RHB RFM
Born 16 July 1973

The son of former Test fast bowler Peter and nephew of batting great Graeme, the young Pollock has shown some of the characteristics of both relatives in a rapid rise up the international rankings. A fast-medium bowler who gains swing and movement off the seam and an ...ant batsman, he has strong claims to be the leading all-...der in world cricket. Pollock achieved the double of 1000 ...s and 100 wickets in only his 26th Test, fourth-fastest of all ...e behind Ian Botham, Vinoo Mankad and Kapil Dev. He was ...a of the match in the first two Tests against the West Indies ...n his bowling set South Africa on the way to an eventual 5-0 ...ewash. He reached the 1000-run/100-wicket double in one-...internationals in only 68 matches, the fastest of all time and ...n matches earlier than Botham.

JONTY RHODES

RHB
Born 27 July 1969

His exuberance and acrobatic fielding during South Africa's first World Cup appearance in 1992 made Jonty Rhodes a national hero. Seven years on, he is nothing short of a global icon. He remains a fielder of extraordinary ability, who continues to stand out in what is overall an excellent fielding team. He acts as an inspiration to his teammates from his favourite backward point position, both through his example and his constant encouragement of other players. He is also a hard-hitting, inventive middle-order batsman who is able to score at close to a run a ball in almost any situation. Although he has always been an automatic choice in the one-day side, he struggled for a while at Test level - but hard work on his technique has given his Test career a new lease of life. He set a world one-day record of five catches against the West Indies in Bombay in 1993-94.

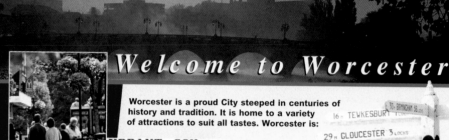

Welcome to Worcester

Worcester is a proud City steeped in centuries of history and tradition. It is home to a variety of attractions to suit all tastes. Worcester is:

A Vibrant City

Quality shopping choices in the modern CrownGate Centre and specialist shopping in historic Friar Street. Restaurants to suit all palates and a selection of pubs and clubs.

A Historic City

1,500 years of history and heritage are preserved and presented. The Commandery Civil War Centre, the impressive Queen Anne Guildhall and the magnificent Cathedral are just some of the historic attractions to visit.

An Attractive City

The timeless attraction of the River Severn flows through the heart of the City and with it a host of riverside diversions.

A Sporting City

Overlooking the riverside in Worcester are two famous sporting venues. One of the oldest racecourses in the country sits close to what is arguably the prettiest cricket ground in the country. The Severn also provides excellent stretches of water for keen anglers.

A City That Entertains

The Worcester Swan Theatre provides year round entertainment, along with a selection of museums and art galleries. Other attractions include Royal Worcester Porcelain, composer Elgar's Birthplace Museum and the ruins of Whitley Court.

For a free guide packed with essential information for every Worcester Visitor ring the Tourist Information Centre on 01905 726311.

CITY OF
WORCESTER
Your City Your Council

Sri Lanka

Complete outsiders last time, but now up there with the favourites. That is the measure of the advance Sri Lankan cricket has made between the 1996 and 1999 World Cups.

No country, however, deserved glory more than underrated Sri Lanka when Arjuna Ranatunga lifted the World Cup trophy on a March night in Lahore, with the Australians trounced by seven wickets.

Rated at 66-1 before the tournament began, and regarded so lightly by many of the top nations that they had been given few Test opportunities since their elevation to full Member status in 1982, Sri Lanka produced intelligent, sparkling and innovative cricket to sweep all before them.

Openers Sanath Jayasuriya and Romesh Kaluwitharana repeatedly savaged the bowling in a series of breathtaking attacks on the new ball, pushing back the boundaries of what was thought possible in the first 15 overs of fielding restrictions.

Further down the order, Aravinda de Silva underlined his status as one of the world's very best batsmen - capping his own triumphant tournament by becoming only the third man, after Clive Lloyd and Viv Richards, to score a World Cup final century. And, in the field, skipper Ranatunga proved himself the master of building pressure on the opposition batsmen.

In short, Sri Lanka had a game plan - and it worked to perfection. This time, however, they may have to come up with something different - as much because of English conditions as because the rest of the world have played tactical catch-up.

Sri Lanka played in the first two World Cups as a non-Test nation, bravely chasing a huge Australian total in 1975 despite various injuries suffered against the frightening pace of Lillee and Thomson, and then in 1979 beating India to record their first significant victory as a coming force.

But they were still eliminated at the group stage at each of the next three World Cup tournaments, because of a lack of incisive bowling.

The rise of Muttiah Muralitharan, as a controversial but potent attacking weapon, and the emergence in Chaminda Vaas of a top-class opening bowler, at last gave Sri Lanka a much-needed balance to their collection of wristy strokeplayers - and the rest is history.

Nine of the side which won in Lahore 38 months ago are in the current 15, with the most notable additions the exciting young batsmen Marvan Atapattu and Mahela Jayawardene.

CRICKET 2000

PARIS

The New Fragrance
For
The New Millennium

Eau
de
Parfum

MADE IN FRANCE

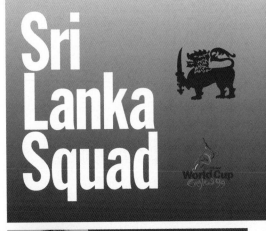

Sri Lanka Squad

ARJUNA RANATUNGA (C)

LHB
Born 1 December 1963

The 'Little General' may be a bit on the portly side these days, but no-one can deny Ranatunga's achievements as an aggressive, inspirational and tactically-astute captain. He lifted the 1996 World Cup of course, after a triumphant tournament full of innovation and ⸍pped by a thumping final victory against the Aussies, but his ⸍acy to Sri Lankan cricket will be much greater even than that. ⸍s an 18-year old, he played in their very first Test, against ⸍gland in 1982, and since then has seen it all. Apart from a ⸍ll in 1992, when Aravinda de Silva took over, he has skippered ⸍e side since 1988 - and dragged Sri Lanka with him into the ⸍g league. Whipping boys no more, they have fought hard for ⸍rld recognition, and Ranatunga has been at the very forefront ⸍ that battle. He is also the only player in this tournament to ⸍ve played in the 1983 World Cup.

MARVAN ATAPATTU

RHB
Born 22 November 1970

Showed tremendous determination to make a fist of a career in international cricket after suffering the trauma of scoring just one run from his first six Test innings, following his debut against India in Chandigarh in 1990-91. But the Sri Lankan selectors stuck by him, and ⸍eir faith has been rewarded. A technically-correct player, ⸍pecially strong down the ground, he is remembered in England ⸍r his magnificent 132 not out in the final of the 1998 Emirates ⸍rophy at Lord's. Played his first one-day international against ⸍dia in 1990-91, at Nagpur.

UPUL CHANDANA

RHB LB
Born 5 July 1972

A classic one-day specialist - a useful, wristy batsman who bowls flattish, quickish leg-spin and is a brilliant ground fielder with a good arm. Made a long-awaited Test debut in March, taking 6-179 as Sri Lanka were beaten by Pakistan in the final of the Asian Test Championship in Dhaka. By the start of this World Cup, however, he already had 51 limited-overs international caps behind him. Made his debut, against Australia, in the 1993-94 Australasia Cup in Sharjah. Ran out Alec Stewart with a lightning pick-up-and-throw during Sri Lanka's epic Test victory against England at The Oval last August. He was the substitute fielder.

ARAVINDA DE SILVA

RHB OB
Born 17 October 1965

One of only three men to have scored a century in World Cup finals. His brilliant 107 not out in the triumph over Australia in Lahore on March 17, 1996, sent Sri Lankans everywhere into raptures. It also put him on a pedestal alongside Clive Lloyd (102 in 1975) and Viv ⸍ichards (138 not out in 1979). An impish, daring, beautifully-⸍alanced batsman of the highest class, he also played one of the ⸍reat one-day innings in English domestic cricket with a century ⸍ a losing cause for Kent in the 1995 Benson and Hedges Cup ⸍nal at Lord's. A more than useful off-spinner, who also took 3-⸍2 in the 1996 World Cup final to make the man-of-the-match ⸍djudication that day the easiest of tasks.

CHANDIKA HATHURUSINGHE

RHB RM
Born 13 September 1968

A squad player for many years, he has had to take his chances of a place in either the Test or one-day international teams when they have been offered. Has never let Sri Lanka down, and now gets his reward of another World Cup trip. Made 23 and 81 against New Zealand at Hamilton when given his Test debut in 1990-91, and has now won 24 Test caps. Had also chalked up 35 one-day international appearances before this tournament, having made his debut in 1991-92, against Pakistan at Sargodha. Was a member of the 1992 World Cup squad.

SANATH JAYASURIYA
LHB SLA
Born 30 June 1969

A phenomenon who has transformed attitudes in the one-day international game through his incredible hitting at the top of the order. Won the 1996 World Cup quarter-final against England by smashing 82 from just 44 balls - and soon after that tournament hit Pakistan's attack for a 48-ball century in Nairobi. Has been no slouch in the Test arena either. In August 1997 he hit 340 against India at Colombo, the fourth highest Test score of all time, and last August stroked a mesmerising 213 as Sri Lanka out-thought and outplayed England at The Oval. England also remember him taking 6-29 to win a one-day international at Moratuwa in March 1993. It is often forgotten that Jayasuriya, besides his batting pyrotechnics, was also the first Sri Lankan to reach 150 one-day international wickets.

MAHELA JAYAWARDEN
RHB RM
Born 27 May 1977

One of Sri Lanka's fast-emerging new generation, Jayawardene is a strokemaker with the potential to match the deeds, one day, of the lik of De Silva and Ranatunga. Hit 12 against England in the bad-tempered clash in Adelaide during the Carlton and United series earli this year, and made his one-day international debut against Zimbabwe, at Colombo, in 1997-98. Scored 66 on his Test debut, against India at Colombo in 1997 - in the match that Jayasuriya made his 340 and put on a record 576 with Roshan Mahanama. Hit 157 against New Zealand at Galle in mid-199 and a classy 242 against India in February.

RUWAN KALPAGE
RHB OB
Born 19 February 1970

Preferred to 1996 World Cup winner Kumara Dharmasena for this tournament, Kalpage is a highly-experienced off-spinning all-rounder with no less than 86 one-day international caps to his name before the World Cup began. His debut was against Pakistan back in 1991-92, and he has also won 10 Test appearances. A steady if unspectacular lower-order batsman, and a steady if unspectacular bowler too, pushing his off-breaks through at a fair pace and concentrating on accuracy rather than the generation of sharp turn.

ROMESH KALUWITHARAN
RHB WK
Born 24 November 1969

Dashing one-day opener and much improved wicketkeeper with more than 100 one-day international appearances to his credit. Hit the headlines during the last World Cu with his whirlwind starts alongside Jayasuriya. A magnificent striker of the ball, especially for one of such small stature, and is completely unafraid of taking the aerial rou in the early overs. Played his first one-day international as far back as 1990-91, against India at Margoa, and for a while was not a regular member of the squad. But, after hitting a spectacular 132 not out on his Test debut, against Australia at Colombo in 1992-93, he became a valuable part of the emerging Sri Lankan side. Scored exactly 100 against Pakistan in Lahore early March to show his batting powers have not waned.

ROSHAN MAHANAMA
RHB
Born 31 May 1966

Now entering the veteran stage, and very much one of the unsung heroes of Sri Lanka's rise into the big league of world cricket. A specialist Test opener for much of his career, he has been used productively down the order in the one-day game. Before this World Cup he had made a staggering 208 one-day international appearances, scoring more than 5000 runs. Did not bat in Sri Lanka's 1996 World Cup final victory, so in terms of personal achievement his greatest day was making 225 against India in the Colombo Test of August 1997, sharing in the world record stand of 576 with Sanath Jayasuriya. Made both his Test and one-day debuts against Pakistan in 1985-86. Noted for his cover driving, his nimbleness at the crease and his ability in the field.

MUTTIAH MURALITHARAN
RHB OB
Born 17 April 1972

Perhaps the most controversial of modern cricketers, this genius of spin has suffered throughout his career at the hands of those who claim he throws certain deliveries, but his supporters insist his unique, double-jointed twist of his wrist at the point of delivery is the reason fo his excessive turn - and that his arm is slightly bent only because he cannot straighten it totally due to a physical deformity. There is no doubting his incredible accuracy and variety, though. Has already taken more than 200 Test wickets, since his debut in 1992-93, and came into this World Cup with 151 one-day international victims too. Destroyed Sri Lanka's batting twice last August, with a Test match return of 16-220 at The Oval, and then a Lord's best one-day international return of 5-34 in the final of the Emirates Trophy.

HASHAN TILLEKERATNE
LHB OB
Born 14 July 1967

Vastly-experienced, with 180 one-day caps coming into this World Cup. Has been a Test regular, too, since making his debut in 1989, and is Sri Lanka's reserve wicket-keeper in this squad, having begun his career as a specialist gloveman. Can also bowl usefully, in a crisis, but his main service to Sri Lankan cricket over the years has been as a stylish, dependable left-hander and a brilliant fielder in any position. Made his one-day international debut as a 19-year old in the 1986-87 Champions Trophy in Sharjah.

Sri Lanka Squad One-Day Career Averages
Based on all matches played up to 30/04/1999

BATTING AND FIELDING

NAME	M	I	NO	RUNS	HS	AVGE	100	50	CT	ST
P.A.de Silva	254	247	25	8020	145	36.12	11	55	79	-
A.Ranatunga	264	250	47	7320	131*	36.05	4	48	62	-
M.S.Atapattu	69	68	8	2028	132*	33.80	2	14	28	-
H.P.Tillekeratne	180	153	38	3438	104	29.89	2	12	79	6
R.S.Mahanama	208	193	23	5026	119*	29.56	4	35	108	-
S.T.Jayasuriya	178	170	7	4672	151*	28.66	7	29	59	-
D.P.M.Jayawardene	20	20	2	510	120	28.33	2	2	8	-
U.C.Hathurusinghe	35	33	1	669	66	20.90	-	4	6	-
R.S.Kalpage	86	69	28	844	51	20.58	-	1	33	-
R.S.Kaluwitharana	112	108	6	1930	100*	18.92	1	12	74	49
U.D.U.Chandana	51	40	7	561	50	17.00	-	1	28	-
W.P.U.J.C.Vaas	108	64	22	506	33	12.04	-	-	18	-
E.A.Upashantha	5	4	1	28	15	9.33	-	-	2	-
G.P.Wickremasinghe	111	49	17	238	21*	7.43	-	-	17	-
M.Muralitharan	110	49	23	151	18	5.80	-	-	53	-

ERIK UPASHANTHA
RHB RFM
Born 10 June 1972

Opens the bowling for his club Colts with Chaminda Vaas, and is predominantly a swing bowler. The last of his five one-day international appearances, coming into this World Cup, was in 1995-96 - but he recently made his Test debut against India in the Asian Test Championship. Earned his place in the squad, as back-up for Vaas and Wickremasinghe, with a series of impressive performances in Sri Lankan domestic cricket during the past few months. Has a career-best haul of 8-67, for Colts against the Singhalese Sports Club, and was born in Kurunegala.

BOWLING

NAME	O	M	R	W	AVGE	BEST	5W	ECON
H.P.Tillekeratne	30	1	141	6	23.50	1-3	-	4.70
W.P.U.J.C.Vaas	870.4	82	3677	136	27.03	4-20	-	4.22
M.Muralitharan	995.3	47	4221	151	27.95	5-23	2	4.24
E.A.Upashantha	39	3	182	6	30.33	2-24	-	4.66
U.D.U.Chandana	318.1	3	1569	48	32.68	4-31	-	4.93
S.T.Jayasuriya	1097.5	13	5349	152	35.19	6-29	2	4.87
P.A.de Silva	658.5	16	3240	83	39.03	4-45	-	4.91
G.P.Wickremasinghe	795.1	47	3551	89	39.89	4-48	-	4.46
R.S.Kalpage	660	20	2975	73	40.75	4-36	-	4.50
A.Ranatunga	785	21	3757	79	47.55	4-14	-	4.78
U.C.Hathurusinghe	159	9	709	14	50.64	4-57	-	4.45
D.P.M.Jayawardene	40	0	233	1	233.00	1-24	-	5.82
R.S.Mahanama	0.2	0	7	0	-	-	-	21.00
M.S.Atapattu	8.3	0	41	0	-	-	-	4.82

CHAMINDA VAAS
LHB LFM
Born 27 January 1974

A top-class left-arm seamer who has led the Sri Lankan attack with energy and verve since following a one-day international bow in 1993-94, against India at Rajkot, with a Test debut against Pakistan at Kandy in 1994-95. It is perhaps no coincidence that Sri Lanka's rapid rise as a world power has followed Vaas' introduction as a pace bowler who commands respect. Became the first Sri Lankan to take a Test match haul of 10 wickets, his 10-90 helping his side beat New Zealand by 241 runs at Napier in March 1995. Needed a lengthy break from cricket last year, however, to recover from back trouble. Played in the 1996 World Cup winning team, and began this tournament with 107 one-day caps to his name. A useful tail-end batsman.

PRAMODYA WICKREMASINGHE
RHB RFM
Born 14 August 1971

A willing workhorse with the new ball for many years, Wickremasinghe makes up for a lack of pace with heart, accuracy and the ability to swing the ball away from the right-hander. Has supported Vaas faithfully, and before that struggled manfully with the task of leading Sri Lanka's pace attack largely on his own. Played his first one-day international in 1990-91, against Bangladesh at Calcutta in the Asia Cup, and won a Test debut against Pakistan at Sialkot in 1991-92. Yet another Sri Lankan with happy memories of the 1996 World Cup final win and, before this tournament, the experience of more than 100 one-day international appearances.

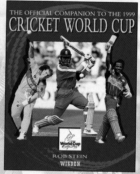

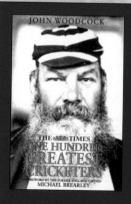

Zimbabwe (Group A)

Possibly the best all-round fielding side in the tournament, even compared with South Africa, but Zimbabwe will be more keen to show they can compete with the best with both bat and ball in hand too.

World cricket's newest Test nation, Zimbabwe were upgraded in July 1992 and have improved steadily and often spectacularly since.

In one-day internationals, certainly, they are far from pushovers - and there are signs that major advancements at Test level are also just around the corner.

Grass roots development has been an almost immediate success, and the rise to prominence of black fast bowlers Henry Olonga and Pom' Mbwanga - amongst others - is proof of a fast-growing awareness of cricket in sections of the community which for years regarded the game as merely the sport of the white farmer.

The return from exile, in Australia and South Africa respectively, of Zimbabwe-born pair Murray Goodwin and Neil Johnson, has also given Zimbabwean cricket a massive boost since the last World Cup.

Eddo Brandes, the chicken-farming fast bowler who took 4-21 to shock England at Albury during the 1992 World Cup, has made this current squad too - alongside familiar and respected names like Heath Streak, Paul Strang, skipper Alistair Campbell and the Flower brothers, Andy and Grant.

Zimbabwe, then of course an associate member country, could not have made a more impressive World Cup entry when they appeared, for the first time, in the 1983 tournament.

Duncan Fletcher, their captain, hit 69 not out and then took 4-42 as Australia were beaten in sensational style by 13 runs at Trent Bridge. Nine days later, at Tunbridge Wells, only an astonishing innings of 175 not out by Kapil Dev prevented Zimbabwe from shocking eventual winners India too.

After that entrance, and remembering that in their 1983 World Cup squad were class players like Dave Houghton, Kevin Curran, Andy Pycroft, John Traicos and Peter Rawson, plus a certain Graeme Hick, then aged 17, it is shameful to record that it took another nine years before Zimbabwe was given the go-ahead to join the Test-playing family. Houghton is now the Zimbabweans' coach, and former left-arm paceman Malcolm Jarvis is this World Cup squad's manager.

•

island cricKit

**Suppliers of probably the finest
cricket bat in the world.
Entirely handcrafted from cleft to finish.**

THE
complete
COLLECTION

Contact
Units 6 & 7, Old Marketfield Industrial Estate, Witheridge, Tiverton, Devon, EX16 8TA
Telephone 01884 860289 Fax: 01884 860062 email: islandcrickit@easynet.co.uk
NOW ON THE WORLDWIDE INTERNET AT: www.web-marketing.co.uk/islandcrikit

Zimbabwe Squad

World Cup

ALISTAIR CAMPBELL (C)

LHB OB
Born 23 September 1972

His father Iain, headmaster at one of Zimbabwe's leading schools, insisted that his son should learn to bat left-handed when a youngster - despite the fact he is a natural right hander. The result is a swashbuckling top-order batsman who uses his dominant top hand to sometimes eye-catching effect. ...air was a schoolboy cricketer of precocious talent and he became ...oungest Zimbabwean to make a first-class century when playing ...st a touring Glamorgan side in 1990. He played for Zimbabwe's ...nal side when still at school, and at 20 made his Test debut in his ...try's historic inaugural Test against India in 1992-93. Before that, ...19, he was entrusted with batting number three in the 1992 ...ld Cup. In Pakistan, in 1993-94, he demonstrated his ability ...st the best when averaging 41 in a three-Test series. He became ...babwe's vice-captain in Australia in 1994-95 and took over as ...in for the 1996-97 home series against England.

EDDO BRANDES

RHB RFM
Born 5 March 1963

The celebrated chicken farmer from the outskirts of Harare made his international debut, against New Zealand, during the 1987 World Cup. Had made 56 one-day international appearances for Zimbabwe, before this tournament, but in recent years has often been ...nt with injury problems. Nevertheless, he is still in there ...ing away for his fourth World Cup, and with the new ball he ...ains a potent force. Was man-of-the-match in Zimbabwe's ...ous World Cup win against England at Albury, in 1992, ...ding old schoolfriend Graeme Hick among his four-wicket ...Took a hat-trick to inspire another win against England at ...are in 1996-97. Made his Test debut in Zimbabwe's ...gural Test, against India, in 1992.

STUART CARLISLE

RHB
Born 10 May 1972

A top-order batsman who made his Test debut against Pakistan in Harare in 1994-95, waiting 11 hours to bat while the Flower brothers shared an epic partnership (and didn't get in), and who played one Test against England in 1996. A prolific run-scorer in school and club cricket, he represented Zimbabwe Schools on tour to Australia (1988 and 1991) and England (1989). Has scored 208 runs in 12 limited-overs international appearances, and is also a fine fielder.

ANDY FLOWER

LHB WK
Born 28 April 1968

One of the most underrated cricketers on the world stage, the elder Flower is a former Zimbabwe captain and perhaps the best specialist wicket-batsman in the game. Has scored more than 2000 runs from his 33 Tests at the outstanding average of 43.54 and ...7 runs in 105 one-day international appearances, before this ...rld Cup. A stylish batsman, with a good range of strokes, he ...lso an accomplished gloveman. Led Zimbabwe to their first ...t win, against Pakistan in 1994-95, and is particularly active ...elping to promote cricket to all sections of the community in ...native country. Made his first-class debut for a Zimbabwe ...cket Union XI against the West Indies in 1986-87, and has ...n a central figure in Zimbabwean cricket ever since.

GRANT FLOWER

RHB SLA
Born 20 December 1970

Had scored 3080 runs from his 92 one-day internationals before this World Cup, averaging more than 35, and has reached at least a half-century in more than 25 per cent of his limited-overs innings. His role is to provide a top-order anchor, and he is perfectly equipped with the technique and the tenacity to do it. The younger brother of Andy, with whom he has shared some memorable partnerships, he has blossomed in recent years from the stodgy, one-paced opener who first emerged when Zimbabwe were admitted into Test cricket in 1992. Made a Test double hundred against Pakistan at Harare in 1994 and, in September 1997, scored a century in each innings of the First Test against New Zealand, also in Harare. A brilliant fielder in any position, he is also a useful slow left-arm spinner - as his 41 one-day international wickets, before this tournament, prove.

MURRAY GOODWIN

RHB
Born 11 December 1972

Zimbabwean cricket was given a major boost 18 months ago when Goodwin decided, like the prodigal, to return to the country of his birth in order to pursue a Test career. It was a sound decision for he now averages 53 in Tests besides scoring 846 runs from 31 one-day internationals, before this World Cup. Goodwin, a class act at the crease, emigrated from his native Harare at the age of 14 - his family settling in Perth. He made his Western Australia debut in 1994-95, hitting 91 and 77 against the touring England side. His Test debut came against Sri Lanka in 1997-98, and he scored 42 and 44 in Zimbabwe's win against India at Harare in October 1998. Six months earlier, at the Bulawayo Test against Pakistan, he hit 166 not out from 204 balls and figured in a record Zimbabwe stand of 277 with Andy Flower.

ADAM HUCKLE

RHB LB
Born 21 September 1971

In recent times leg-spinner Huckle has been preferred to the more experienced Paul Strang as his country's premier slow bowler in cricket, which is testimony to the strides he has made since making debut against New Zealand at Harare in September 1997. Born Bulawayo, but partly-educated in South Africa, Huckle has now settled down into a promising international career which also included, before this World Cup, 16 one-day appearances.

NEIL JOHNSON

LHB RFM
Born 24 January 1970

An all-rounder of true international class who, like Goodwin, has returned to his roots to give Zimbabwean cricket a huge lift. Born in Harare, he grew up in South Africa and played both for Natal and South Africa A, as well as having a season as Leicestershire's overseas player in 1997, in which he topped the county's batting averages with 819 championship runs at an average of 63. He hit his first hundred for Zimbabwe in the one-day win against Pakistan in Sheikhupura in November 1998, and a month earlier he had celebrated his Test debut by dismissing Sachin Tendulkar twice as Zimbabwe beat India in Harare.

MPUMELELO MBANGW

RHB RFM
Born 26 June 1976

An accurate, dependable seamer s learning his trade but already an invaluable member of Zimbabwe's one-day squad. Universally known 'Pom', Mbangwa has been coache both by Dennis Lillee in Madras Clive Rice in South Africa. Befor this World Cup he had played 15 one-day internationals, the first of them against Pakistan, in Lahore, in November 1996. His Test debut had come at Faisalabad a month earlier and that experience at the tender ag of 20 has stood him in good stead.

HENRY OLONGA

RHB RFM
Born 3 July 1976

Made his first-class debut for Matabeleland at the age of 17 in March 1994 - and 10 months later was making his first Test appearance for Zimbabwe in their historic first Test win, against Pakistan. Was the first black cricketer to represent Zimbabwe, but happily looks now to have been at the head of a lengthy conveyor belt of new talent. Called for throwing in a Test in early 1995, he has rebuilt his action and become an even better bowler with lengthy international experience. He took 5-70 against India at Harare in October 1998 and, mainly due to his match-winning burst of 4-42 in Peshawar, was named man-of-the-series when Zimbabwe beat Pakistan for an historic first series win last December. In one-day terms has proved expensive, but is very much a wicket-taker in all forms of cricket.

PAUL STRANG

RHB LB
Born 28 July 1970

A very experienced and accurate le spinner, perhaps not destined to be in the class of either Warne, Mushtaq or Kumble, but still a hu asset to Zimbabwe in their first decade as a full Test-playing natio Took 57 wickets in his first 20 Tes and is also a good enough batsman to have a Test hundred next to his name. In one-day internationals he had taken 79 wickets from 72 matches before this World Cup but, as important, his economy rate is just over four runs per over - a fine record for a bowler of his type. Has much experience of English conditions too, after spells in count cricket with Kent (1997) and Nottinghamshire (1998). A doughty opponent, with a good wrong 'un!

HEATH STREAK

RHB RFM
Born 16 March 1974

Must be classed as a genuine all-rounder and, at 25, with the time to develop still further. Streak represented Zimbabwe Under 19's at rugby but this talented all-round sportman, the son of Denis Streak who played for Zimbabwe from 1976-85, is now concentrating very h on his cricket. Has been in the top 10 bowling rankings for t of his Test career, after making his debut against Pakistan in achi in 1993-94, and is currently ranked eighth with 106 kets from his 26 Tests. Nevertheless, and despite playing for npshire in 1995, Streak is perhaps the most underrated of all world's leading bowlers. Before this World Cup he had also esented Zimbabwe in 73 one-day interanationals, and leads race to become the first Zimbabwean to reach 100 limited-rs international wickets. (He was the first to get to 100 in ts). He is also a capable batsman in a lengthy Zimbabwe ing order.

DIRK VILJOEN

LHB SLA
Born 11 March 1977

Was voted Zimbabwe's Young Cricketer of the Year in 1996-97, and benefitted a lot by attending the Adelaide Cricket Academy in 1997. Viljoen built up a prolific record as a schoolboy, and had three years in the Zimbabwe Under 19 team. An opening batsman by preference, he de a double century in 1996 and made the jump to Test cket last year. His debut came against Pakistan at Bulawayo l, before this tournament, he had won 12 one-day ernational caps. One of a crop of talented young players being ed into the top flight by Zimbabwe, and he will gain much erience by being involved in a World Cup campaign.

Zimbabwe Squad One-Day Career Averages
Based on all matches played up to 30/04/1999

BATTING AND FIELDING

NAME	M	I	NO	RUNS	HS	AVGE	100	50	CT	ST
G.W.Flower	92	90	4	3079	140	35.80	3	22	37	-
N.C.Johnson	14	14	0	500	103	35.71	2	2	7	-
A.Flower	105	103	6	3197	115*	32.95	1	27	75	24
A.D.R.Campbell	97	93	9	2484	131*	29.57	3	15	39	-
M.W.Goodwin	31	31	0	846	111	27.29	1	4	8	-
P.A.Strang	72	59	21	955	47	25.13	-	-	22	-
G.J.Whittall	72	72	10	1509	83	24.33	-	9	18	-
H.H.Streak	73	61	23	809	59	21.28	-	1	15	-
S.V.Carlisle	12	12	2	208	43	20.80	-	-	6	-
D.P.Viljoen	12	11	2	148	36	16.44	-	-	3	-
E.A.Brandes	56	39	9	383	55	12.76	-	2	10	-
A.R.Whittall	44	24	11	141	29	10.84	-	-	12	-
H.K.Olonga	7	2	1	6	6	6.00	-	-	2	-
M.Mbangwa	15	7	2	24	11	4.80	-	-	2	-
A.G.Huckle	16	6	4	9	5*	4.50	-	-	6	-

BOWLING

NAME	O	M	R	W	AVGE	BEST	5W	ECON
H.H.Streak	605.3	48	2672	89	30.02	5-32	1	4.41
P.A.Strang	574.1	32	2383	79	30.16	5-21	2	4.15
E.A.Brandes	450.2	37	2158	69	31.27	5-28	2	4.79
G.W.Flower	266.4	2	1320	41	32.19	4-32	-	4.95
A.D.R.Campbell	57.3	3	259	8	32.37	2-22	-	4.50
D.P.Viljoen	47	0	207	6	34.50	2-31	-	4.40
G.J.Whittall	365.3	8	1899	49	38.75	3-43	-	5.19
H.K.Olonga	46	1	314	8	39.25	4-46	-	6.82
A.R.Whittall	374.1	14	1567	38	41.23	3-23	-	4.18
N.C.Johnson	92.3	4	466	9	51.77	2-39	-	5.03
M.W.Goodwin	34.2	1	173	3	57.66	1-12	-	5.03
M.Mbangwa	116.1	6	569	7	81.28	2-24	-	4.89
A.G.Huckle	123	3	584	6	97.33	2-27	-	4.74
A.Flower	5	0	23	0	-	-	-	4.60

ANDREW WHITTALL

RHB OB
Born 28 March 1973

The younger by almost seven months of the two Whittall cousins, Andrew is a former Cambridge University cricket blue who played under John Crawley's captaincy. He later captained Cambridge himself in the 1994 Varsity match, scoring 91 not out. Made his Test debut against Lanka at Colombo in 1996-97 and, although never sure of a ular place in the Test team, he had won 44 one-day ernational caps by the start of this World Cup. Another steady former with his off-spin, and very much part of Zimbabwe's npetitive and fast-improving squad. A useful tailend batsman.

GUY WHITTALL

RHB RFM
Born 5 September 1972

An all-rounder with the ability to do something extraordinary. The older of the two Whittall cousins is now a very experienced cricketer, though he is not 27 until later this year. His combative medium pace helps to give Zimbabwe's one-day side extra balance and depth, but it is with the bat that he has made the most significant contributions to Zimbabwe's young life as a Test-playing nation. Made his Test debut in 1993-94 and, in February 1995, scored a century in Zimbabwe's historic first Test win, against Pakistan in Harare. Then, in September 1997, came a brilliant 203 not out in the Bulawayo Test against New Zealand. Made his first-class debut back in 1990, for Young Zimbabwe against Pakistan B. At the start of the World Cup he had amassed 72 one-day international appearances.

LEICESTERSHIRE COUNTY CRICKET CLUB

JOIN THE COUNTY CHAMPIONS
FOR CORPORATE ENTERTAINMENT
AND INDIVIDUAL MEMBERSHIP

1ST CLASS FACILITIES
1ST CLASS ENTERTAINMENT
1ST CLASS CATERING & BANQUETING

FOR FURTHER INFORMATION CALL
0116 283 2128

Australia (Group B)

Australia have a surprisingly patchy record in the six previous World Cups, despite winning the 1987 tournament and featuring, in 1975 at Lord's, in the first and best of the finals.

Eliminated at the group stage at both the 1979 and 1983 World Cups, the last two to be held in England, they also failed to get beyond the preliminary round when they co-hosted the event with New Zealand in 1992.

But, since losing to Sri Lanka in the 1996 final, Australia have tinkered further with the make-up of their one-day side and with the tactics they use in the limited-overs arena.

The Aussies were the first nation to approach one-day selection as a completely different exercise to Test cricket, even dropping their then captain Mark Taylor to accommodate another batsman they felt was more in tune with the demands of the short sprint.

Powerful batting lies at the heart of the Australian one-day effort, and in Glenn McGrath they have the most battle-hardened and effective opening bowler in the world. The Waugh twins, McGrath, Shane Warne and Michael Bevan remain from 1996 as the basis of their one-day strength.

Adam Gilchrist, the wicketkeeper-batsman, has however emerged in recent times as a specialist one-day opener of murderous ability, and Ricky Ponting's fielding brilliance has earned him comparison even with Jonty Rhodes. The selection of three specialist one-day seam bowling all-rounders in Shane Lee, Brendon Julian and the veteran Tom Moody underlines Australia's campaign strategy. Leg-spinner Warne, vice-captain to Steve Waugh and miffed to say the least at being dropped from Australia's final Test Indies in early April, will be desperate to prove a point, too.

Australia, indeed, are worthy second favourites behind South Africa, and they are managed by Steve Bernard and coached by Geoff Marsh, their former opener who played 50 Tests between 1985 and 1991.

Marsh was a member of the 1987 World Cup winning team, when Mike Gatting's England were beaten by seven runs in Calcutta. David Boon was man-of-the-match with 75, and a junior member of Allan Border's triumphant side that November day was one S R Waugh.

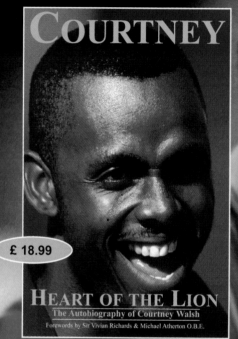

STEVE WAUGH (C)

RHB RM
Born 2 June 1965

No doubt about it - here is the toughest of modern-day cricketers in terms of commitment, attitude and performance. Waugh's sheer technical ability as a batsman is often underrated; but what is clear to the world is his uncompromising outlook. He stares down bowlers and ⁣Test cricket has proved to be the hardest batsman of all to shift ⁣rom the crease. Also a considerable force in one-day cricket, ⁣ven if his clever bowling is not the force of old. The elder twin, ⁣y four minutes, of Mark - who took five years longer to make ⁣he Australian team. Raised in a sports-mad family in the Sydney ⁣uburbs, both he and Mark were playing for the New South ⁣Vales Youth team by the age of 15. Only Allan Border has ⁣cored more Test runs for Australia, but after making his debut at ⁣⁣0 he took almost four years and 26 Tests to reach his first ⁣undred.

Australia Squad

MICHAEL BEVAN

LHB SLC
Born 8 May 1970

Perhaps the most effective middle-order batsman currently playing one-day international cricket. Bevan's rate of scoring, and his consistency, have been quite extraordinary during the past five years. He first sprang to prominence when he became the first player to hit five successive ⁣enturies in Sheffield Shield competition in 1990-91. Scored 82 ⁣n his Test debut, against Pakistan in Karachi in 1994-95 and ⁣ook a match haul of 10-113 when the West Indies were ⁣amboozled by his rich mix of chinamen and googlies in 1996-⁣⁣7. But his Test career has been troubled by a weakness against ⁣hort-pitched fast bowling. Limited-overs cricket, though, is a ⁣lifferent story and Bevan - boosted by a knowledge of English ⁣onditions picked up during two seasons with Yorkshire and one ⁣vith Sussex - could be one of the stars of this World Cup.

ADAM DALE

LHB RM
Born 30 December 1968

Has emerged as a potent force with the new ball, his accuracy and skill making him a distinct threat in helpful conditions as well as tying down good players in the crucial first 15-over phase of the one-day game. Dale holds just one Test cap, won against India in 1997, but he has been a regular in Australia's one-day side for some time now. In the Carlton and United series earlier this year, which Australia won against England and Sri Lanka, Dale's total of 94 overs cost just 313 runs - making him easily the most economical of all the bowlers on show in the competition at 3.32 runs per over. A late bloomer who did not make his first-class debut for Queensland until he was 28. Called "another Terry Alderman" by former Australian captain Allan Border after Dale had captured 25 wickets in last year's Aussie A tour of Scotland and Ireland: nine of his scalps were lbw, seven were bowled and six caught behind. Like Alderman, he bowls from stump to stump.

DAMIEN FLEMING

RHB RFM
Born 24 April 1970

In October 1994, against Pakistan in Rawalpindi, Fleming became only the third player in history to take a hat-trick on his Test debut. Later that winter he took 10 wickets in three Tests against England and seemed set for a lengthy run in the Australian Test side. But a shoulder ⁣njury interrupted his career and it was not until last winter, ⁣vhen he took 16 wickets in four Tests against England, that he ⁣returned to the side. Fleming's ability to swing the ball both ⁣vays makes him a dangerous customer, and in English ⁣conditions his control of seam movement too will add to his ⁣armoury. A more than handy late-order hitter. He is also a ⁣patriotic man: when recalled to the Test stage at Brisbane last ⁣November he draped his Aussie blazer over his bed the night ⁣before the game as extra motivation.

ADAM GILCHRIST

LHB WK
Born 14 November 1971

Highly-effective batsman at the top of Australia's one-day batting order, as demonstrated by his 129-ball 154 against Sri Lanka at Melbourne in February. It was the highest one-day international score by an Australian, and contained 14 fours and four sixes. In all, during that Carlton and United series, Gilchrist scored 525 runs from 12 innings at 43.75, but perhaps more importantly at a staggering strike rate of 98.13 runs per 100 balls faced. Toured England with Young Australia in 1995, topping the batting averages with 495 runs at 61.87, and made his Sheffield Shield breakthrough with New South Wales. But he soon decided to move to Western Australia and in the 1995-96 season claimed a record 54 dismissals besides hitting 189 not out in the Shield final.

BRENDON JULIAN

RHB LFM
Born 10 August 1970

Western Australian all-rounder of Polynesian descent, Julian is a handy cricketer to have around. Fitted in well at Surrey in 1996, scoring 759 runs (including his first two first-class centuries) and taking 61 wickets. His knowledge of English conditions has been enhanced by selection for the past two Ashes tours, in 1993 and 1997. Won the man-of-the-match award on his one-day international debut, at Lord's in 1993. Made his Test debut later on that tour at Old Trafford, scoring a half-century to help Steve Waugh mount a successful rearguard action in a drawn match. Not a regular member of Australia's side at either Test or one-day level, but an important squad player. Does a bit of boxing in his spare time to keep his reflexes sharp.

SHANE LEE

RHB RM
Born 8 August 1973

A robust all-rounder from New South Wales, who has often promised more than he has delivered. But he seemed to turn a corner last winter, taking 5-33 against Sri Lanka and also averaging 24 with the bat in the Carlton and United series against England and the Sri Lankans. Two huge sixes off England's Alan Mullally in the 50th over of the second one-day final demonstrated his ability as a hitter. Lee also averaged 61 with the bat during his one season in county cricket, with Somerset in 1996. His bowling has improved markedly in recent years, and he now has a deceptive slower ball which he learned by watching Steve Waugh do it in a televised match!

DARREN LEHMANN

LHB SLA
Born 5 February 1970

Dubbed 'the new Bradman' in his early years, when it was obvious he had a special talent, Lehmann has only recently begun to shake off the memory of that unwanted burden and establish himself as a bold, powerful striker of the ball with an eye-catchingly uncomplicated style. Made his first-class debut for South Australia as long ago as 1987-88 and, after a three-year fling with Victoria, returned to play for his native state in 1993-94. Hit 255 against Queensland in 1996-97 and, for the past two seasons, has proved a huge hit as Yorkshire's overseas player. Was first named in an Australian Test squad in 1989-90, when 19, but he did not actually make his Test debut until 1997, when he scored 52 against India in Bangalore.

DAMIEN MARTYN

RHB
Born 21 October 1971

A naturally-talented strokemaker who is currently having a second bite at life as a member of Australia's one-day elite. Martyn's career had seemed to grind to a halt after the last of his seven Tests in 1993-94 - despite great success on the 1993 Ashes tour of England in which he scored 838 runs at an average of 69.83. But greater maturity and several productive seasons with Western Australia earned him a recall in 1998 and - given an extended opportunity because of injury to Steve Waugh - he responded with 290 runs at an average of 58 in the Carlton and United series against England and Sri Lanka. This return of confidence at the top level made sure of his World Cup berth, and he now has the chance of fulfilling the early promise he showed at the Australian Academy and as captain of the Australian Under 19 team.

TOM MOODY

RHB RM
Born 2 October 1965

'Long Tom' has played well over 50 one-day internationals, but only eight Tests. Those were between 1989 to 1992, and since 1995 Moody has concentrated more on his double responsibilities as captain both of Worcestershire and his equally beloved Western Australia. Played one season for Warwickshire in 1990, after impressing them by scoring a century against the county for the 1989 touring Australians. Joined Worcestershire in 1991 and has long been regarded as part of the furniture at New Road. First played for Western Australia as long ago as 1985-86, and his ability as a stroke-making batsman is underlined by the 272 he made for them against Tasmania in 1994-95. His clever, accurate medium-pace - which is especially effective in English conditions - is another good reason for his inclusion in this World Cup squad. Took part in the 1996 World Cup.

GLENN McGRATH

RHB RF
Born 9 February 1970

Known as The Enforcer, and - on the field - as mean a fast bowler as there has ever been. Don't the Aussies just love him. A world-class performer and the modern successor of a line stretching back through Dennis Lillee and Ray Lindwall to the legendary Fred Spofforth, the 'Demon' of the 1870's and 1880's. Tall and lean, he preferred basketball to cricket until he was 16. Soon this country boy with mental and physical hardness was emerging from the bush to live in a caravan while he broke into the New South Wales team. Within a year, though, he was playing Test cricket and in early 1995 sprang to worldwide attention by spearheading Australia's great triumph in the West Indies. His 8-38 in 1997 are the best figures by an Australian at Lord's. Took his 100th wicket in his 23rd Test (equalling Shane Warne and bettering Lillee by one) and his 200th in his 45th Test. Unrelenting, he just gets better and better.

RICKY PONTING
RHB RM
Born 19 Decemeber 1974

One of the many products of the Adelaide Academy, this gifted young batsman was earmarked for greatness from a very young age. Scored 96 on his Test debut against Sri Lanka at Perth in 1995, falling only to a controversial lbw decision. Made 88 against the West Indies in 1996-97 then lost form and was dropped. Recalled for the 1997 Ashes ⸱es, he responded with 127 in the Fourth Test at Headingley had a series average of 48. Did well in the recent Test series ⸱Vest Indies, and is almost in the Jonty Rhodes class as a ⸱nd fielder. Has an impressive one-day international record, hit a century against the West Indies in the 1996 World ⸱. Known affectionately as 'Punter' because of his fondness for ⸱ing.

Australia Squad One-Day Career Averages
Based on all matches played up to 30/04/1999
BATTING AND FIELDING

NAME	M	I	NO	RUNS	HS	AVGE	100	50	CT	ST
M.G.Bevan	104	93	37	3484	108ⁿ	62.21	3	24	39	-
R.T.Ponting	73	73	8	2566	145	39.47	5	14	19	-
M.E.Waugh	181	176	13	6261	130	38.41	11	40	70	-
A.C.Gilchrist	58	56	4	1861	154	35.78	5	6	66	13
D.S.Lehmann	45	43	6	1311	110ⁿ	35.43	2	7	7	-
S.R.Waugh	258	235	45	5840	102ⁿ	30.73	1	35	87	-
D.R.Martyn	33	30	6	629	59ⁿ	26.20	-	3	7	-
T.M.Moody	63	56	6	1071	89	21.42	-	9	17	-
A.C.Dale	24	9	6	56	15ⁿ	18.66	-	-	9	-
S.Lee	23	20	4	286	47	17.87	-	-	12	-
P.R.Reiffel	86	55	21	502	58	14.76	-	1	24	-
B.P.Julian	23	16	0	215	35	13.43	-	-	8	-
S.K.Warne	115	69	21	596	55	12.41	-	1	40	-
D.W.Fleming	51	17	11	32	5ⁿ	5.33	-	-	7	-
G.D.McGrath	86	27	15	49	10	4.08	-	-	11	-

BOWLING

NAME	O	M	R	W	AVGE	BEST	5W	ECON
D.W.Fleming	446.5	32	1976	82	24.09	5-36	1	4.42
S.K.Warne	1075.2	61	4490	182	24.67	5-33	1	4.17
G.D.McGrath	768.5	84	3085	122	25.28	5-40	2	4.01
P.R.Reiffel	731.4	81	2858	99	28.86	4-13	-	3.90
S.Lee	134.3	8	622	21	29.61	5-33	1	4.62
A.C.Dale	212	24	821	27	30.40	3-18	-	3.87
M.E.Waugh	549.3	11	2614	81	32.27	5-24	1	4.75
S.R.Waugh	1427.2	56	6471	187	34.60	4-33	-	4.53
M.G.Bevan	254.2	3	1258	31	40.58	3-36	-	4.94
B.P.Julian	174	9	917	22	41.68	3-40	-	5.27
T.M.Moody	368.1	18	1631	38	42.92	3-39	-	4.43
D.S.Lehmann	67	0	359	8	44.87	2-11	-	5.35
R.T.Ponting	14	0	62	1	62.00	1-41	-	4.42
D.R.Martyn	24.4	0	128	1	128.00	1-30	-	5.18

PAUL REIFFEL
RHB RFM
Born 19 April 1966

A proven threat in English conditions, following his success here in both the 1993 and 1997 Ashes series. Now 33, Reiffel seems to have lost his Test place to the likes of Jason Gillespie and other younger bloods. But he will be no less dangerous in this World Cup and an enviably low economy rate from a one-day career spanning ⸱re than 80 internationals. Took eight wickets on his Ashes ⸱ut in 1993 and eventually finished on top of the Test bowling ⸱rages for that tour with 19 at 20.84 apiece. In recent years he also developed as a more-than-useful late order batsman. ⸱own throughout the game by his nickname 'Pistol', and is ⸱versally respected as a high-class 'stock' bowler.

SHANE WARNE
RHB LB
Born 13 September 1969

One of the true greats of cricket history, not just for his Test and one-day international record but also for the way - in the early 90's - he almost single-handedly raised the stock of leg-spin bowling in the world game. Before the emergence of Warne, the drop-out from the Academy with the ⸱ch-blond highlights, the jangling jewellery and the alluring ⸱ge of the likeable rogue, leg-spinners had become almost ⸱nct as a Test species. Now, thanks to Warne, every nation ⸱king world domination has to have one; witness Anil Kumble's ⸱cess with India, Pakistan's reliance on Mushtaq Ahmed and ⸱gland's repeated gambles with Ian Salisbury. Delivered the so-⸱ed 'ball of the century' to clip Mike Gatting's off bail at Old ⸱fford in 1993; it was Warne's first ball in a Test in England. ⸱erations on both his spinning finger and a troublesome ⸱ulder have bothered him, but he is still mesmerisingly accurate.

MARK WAUGH
RHB OB
Born 2 June 1965

The younger of the Waugh twins, by just four minutes. Displaced Steve to win his first Test cap in 1990-91, five years after his brother, and promptly savaged England's attack for 138 at Adelaide. Since then has established himself as one of Australia's elite batsmen - and certainly one of the most stylish in their long history. Is sometimes so languid at the crease that he is accused of being too casual. The only Australian to have made 3,000 runs in a calendar year and has three passions: food, gambling and sport. He owns racehorses and loves golf.

HOWZAT!

for the best corporate day out for you and your guests.

Northamptonshire County Cricket Club offers excellent facilities for both corporate hospitality and conferences.

Available 365 days a year, our tailored packages are the best all round.

For further information and a copy
of our brochure please call

Nigel Felton
on 01604 514455

**NORTHAMPTONSHIRE
COUNTY CRICKET CLUB**

THE COUNTY GROUND
WANTAGE ROAD NORTHAMPTON NN1 4TJ
TELEPHONE 01604 514455
FACSIMILE 01604 514488
E-MAIL frances.allbury.northants@ecb.co.uk

Bangladesh (Group B)

Their odds for winning the World Cup are 1000-1, which sums up [th]eir chances succinctly, but [the] real prize for Bangladesh [is] likely to come within the [ne]xt 12 months.

Elevation to full Test [sta]tus is on the cards after the [ste]ady progress they have made [sin]ce being awarded official one-day [int]ernational status, and that promotion [co]uld come in the year 2000 if they show well in this World Cup.

Bangladeshi administrators and [pla]yers alike were distraught [ba]ck in 1994 when they [ex]pected to be one of the [thr]ee associate member [co]untries to qualify for [the] 1996 World Cup [to]urnament. But they [we]re beaten at the ICC Trophy [ev]ent by Holland, Kenya and [the] United Arab Emirates - [an]d that trio instead got to mix [with] the big boys.

Now, though, it is [Ba]ngladesh's turn to take a [W]orld Cup bow, and the country literally [we]nt crazy when they beat Scotland in the [se]mi-final of the last ICC Trophy, in 1997, [to] make sure of their qualification.

David Richards, the ICC's chief [ex]ecutive, was given a glimpse of Bangladesh's rich potential as a fully-fledged cricket nation when, in 1993, he witnessed 15,000 spectators turning up to watch a modest league match at Dhaka's National Cricket Stadium.

And worldwide awareness of Bangladesh's love of cricket came last autumn when huge crowds attended the inaugural ICC Knock-Out event - even though the Bangladeshi team was not competing. Visitors from around the globe marvelled too at the organisation, the fine facilities, and the way Bangladesh had fought back from terrible flooding just weeks beforehand to stage the tournament faultlessly.

Coach Gordon Greenidge, the former West Indies opener and a World Cup winner in 1975 and 1979, was granted Bangladeshi citizenship after the ICC Trophy success, and each player was given a new car and mobile phone - huge privileges in the poverty-stricken ninth most populous country on the globe. The team is managed by Tanveer Muzhar Islam.

Come Home To
THE CRICKETERS CLUB OF LONDON

Our friendly private members club is home-from-home for cricketers and those who love the game. In the heart of the West End, we're just 15 minutes from Lord's and five minutes from Baker Street, Bond Street and Marble Arch tube stations.

The Club offers a bright, welcoming Bar in the style of a Victorian pavilion, and a comfortabl Restaurant serving first-class lunch and dinner. The newly opened Denis Compton Room is available for private hire by members and non-members. All at very sensible prices.

The Cricketers Club of London is the ideal meeting place where you can relax in good company. Our unique collection of cricket memorabilia adds to the ambience. You can also catch the major sporting events on our two wide-screen televisions.

We provide a range of activities, including cricket, golf, jazz nights and excursions, for members to enjoy and we keep everyone in touch with our free bi-monthly 'Bats 'n Balls' newsletter.

Annual full membership is just £63 *(you receive £20 of vouchers to spend in the Restaurant)* and, for those who live and work outside London, country membership is just £33 *(includes £10 of vouchers)*. There are small reductions if you pay by Banker's Orde Corporate membership is also available.

Please mention *World Cup 1* when you request a membership application form.

See you at The Cricketers

The Cricketers Club of London
71 Blandford Street, London W1H 3AL

0171 486 2635

President Trevor Bailey CBE Vice Presidents Godfrey Evans (Rachael Heyhoe Flint MBE, Keith Miller MBE

AMINUL ISLAM (C)

RHB OB
Born 2 February 1968

Scored 121 against the touring England A side in Dhaka in early 1995, and for years has been Bangladesh's leading batsman. Also bowls off-spin to a respectable standard. Has succeeded Akram Khan as captain for this tournament and a lot is being asked of him. Made his debut against India at Chittagong in the 1988-89 Asia up and is so popular in cricket-mad Bangladesh that he is own to everyone as 'Bulbul'. A stylish batsman, comfortable ainst top-class pace bowling in contrast to some other of his ammates.

Bangladesh Squad

World Cup

AKRAM KHAN

RHB
Born 1 February 1967

Led Bangladesh to their most famous victory - the 1997 ICC Trophy final triumph against Kenya in Malaysia, the tournament in which they confirmed their qualification for this World Cup. In that match Akram added a vital 53 in nine overs for the fourth wicket with Aminul Islam, and top-scored with 37. A stocky figure, he es his strength to bludgeon rather than caress the bowling. His rm dipped for a while after the excitement of the ICC Trophy, it he returned to his best during the Triangular tournament th Kenya and Zimbabwe in March. Very experienced, having ade his one-day international debut against Pakistan at hittagong, his place of birth, during the 1988-89 Asia Cup.

ENAMUL HOQUE

LHB SLA
Born 27 February 1966

Made his Bangladesh one-day international debut against New Zealand in the 1989-90 Australasia Cup and is nicknamed 'Moni'. A steady left-arm spinner with 16 caps to his credit before the start of this World Cup, but only seven wickets. Enamul is also a useful lower middle-order batsman and was a member of the team that beat Kenya in the 1997 ICC Trophy final in Kuala Lumpur.

FARUQUE AHMED

RHB OB
Born 3 March 1966

Third oldest member of the squad, and made his debut back in 1986. Has been brought back by the Bangladeshi selectors after a lengthy absence with injury problems. Captained Bangladesh at the 1994 ICC Trophy but had made just five one-day international appearances fore this World Cup. His highest score, 58, was made against dia at Chandigarh in 1990. Skippered the Biman club to the emier one-day trophy during the winter. Has a masters degree public administration.

HASIBUL HUSSAIN

RHB RFM
Born 3 June 1977

Was only 17 when he made his Bangladesh debut in the 1994-95 Asia Cup in Sharjah, and with 20 one-day international caps going in to this World Cup has much experience for his age. Bowls at quite a lively pace, although he has problems with no balls and wides. Was at the wicket with Khaled Masud when victory was clinched against Kenya in the ICC Trophy final in 1997, but has no great pretensions with the bat.

KHALED MAHMUD

RHB RM
Born 26 July 1971

One of the smallest men in world cricket at a shade over five foot, he is a medium pacer whose lack of height means he skids the ball on. Took 2-31 from seven overs in the ICC Trophy final, including Kenyan century-maker Steve Tikolo among his two victims. Made his one-day international debut during the 1997-98 Silver Jubilee Independence Cup, against India at Dhaka, and is also a handy late-order batsman with a top score of 47.

KHALED MASUD

RHB WK
Born 8 February 1976

A tidy wicketkeeper who hit a six from the first ball of the last over, bowled by Martin Suji, to set up Bangladesh's dramatic victory in th 1997 ICC Trophy final against Kenya in Malaysia. Masud made h one-day international debut in the 1994-95 Asia Cup, against India a Sharjah, and has been the first-choice keeper ever since. Had won 20 caps before the start of this World Cup. At 23 he has h best years in front of him and should be a central figure in the further development of Bangladeshi cricket.

MANJURUL ISLAM

RHB LM
Born 7 November 1979

Arrived at the World Cup with just a single one-day international appearance to his name, against Pakistan at Dhaka in March. Took the wicket of Wajahatullah Wasti and scored one. He is a student at Dhaka University and lists Wasim Akram and Chaminda Vaas as his role models. If he turns out to be even half as good as the former he will be ensured of everlasting stardom in his cricket-mad country. Stamp collecting is his hobby.

MEHRAB HOSSAIN

RHB RM
Born 22 August 1978

Dhaka-born youngster who is a fas emerging batsman of talent. Won the honour, in late March, of hittin Bangladesh's first century in one-da international competition - against Zimbabwe during the Triangular series in his home city. Small of stature but quick on his feet, both a the crease and in the field. Made his international debut 18 months ago, playing against India at Mohali in the 1997-98 Coca-Cola Triangular series. One of the cricketers Bangladesh i hoping can take them forward as an international force.

MINHAJUL ABEDIN

RHB RM
Born 25 September 1965

Originally omitted from the squad, but then added later at the expense of Jahangir Alam. Minhajul, a batsman who can bowl either seam-up or off-spin, is the most senior player in the squad. He made his debut in the 1985-86 Asia Cup, against Pakistan at Colombo. Captained his country from 1990 to 1994 and, in four ICC Trophy events scored 739 runs and took 38 wickets. Before this World Cup, though, his top score was just 45.

MOHAMMAD RAFIQU

LHB SLA
Born 15 May 1970

Had the experience of 16 previous one-day international caps behind him going into this World Cup, ane is one of Bangladesh's key men. A fine slow left-armer, who took 3-4C in the ICC Trophy final in 1997 an then hit a quickfire 26 as an openin batsman. Took 4-25 in the ICC semi-final win against Scotland. First played for Bangladesh in the 1994-95 Asia Cup event in Sharjah, against India. Celebrate his 29th birthday during the World Cup.

NAIMUR RAHMAN

RHB OB
Born 19 September 1974

A useful off-spinning all-rounder who made his Bangladesh debut against Pakistan at Sharjah in the 1994-95 Asia Cup. Opened the batting during the ICC Trophy final in 1997, but is more likely to come in further down the order these days. Played in the 1997-98 Coca-Cola ,angular series and had 11 caps coming in to this tournament. competent fielder in a side which is not noted for its ability in it department.

NEEYAMUR RASHID

RHB RM
Born 1 January 1975

A new face who had made only one appearance for Bangladesh before this World Cup, scoring four not out and taking 1-48 against Zimbabwe in Dhaka in March. Won his selection for this squad on the strength of his successes with championship-winning club ahani in Bangladesh's premier league cricket. A fine fielder h close to the wicket and in the deep. Was born in Pabna.

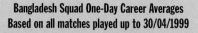
BATTING AND FIELDING

NAME	M	I	NO	RUNS	HS	AVGE	100	50	CT	ST
Mehrab Hossain	5	5	0	207	101	41.40	1	1	1	-
Aminul Islam	26	26	5	566	70	26.95	-	2	9	-
Akram Khan	26	26	2	618	65	25.75	-	4	6	-
Shahriar Hossain	10	10	0	214	95	21.40	-	2	4	-
Khaled Mahmud	11	10	0	188	47	18.80	-	-	1	-
Faruque Ahmed	5	5	0	89	57	17.80	-	1	1	-
Mohammad Rafique	13	13	0	215	77	16.53	-	1	3	-
Naimur Rahman	12	12	1	170	47	15.45	-	-	5	-
Minhajul Abedin	23	22	0	313	45	14.22	-	-	2	-
Khaled Masud	20	18	4	155	27'	11.07	-	-	16	2
Enamul Hoque	16	14	3	91	18	8.27	-	-	3	-
Hasibul Hussain	20	17	2	122	21'	8.13	-	-	4	-
Shafiuddin Ahmed	8	7	4	17	11	5.66	-	-	-	-
Neeyamur Rashid	1	1	1	4	4'	-	-	-	1	-
Manjural Islam	1	1	1	1	1'	-	-	-	-	-

BOWLING

NAME	O	M	R	W	AVGE	BEST	5W	ECON
Shafiuddin Ahmed	62.3	3	303	10	30.30	3-42	-	4.84
Khaled Mahmud	87.4	5	382	11	34.72	2-12	-	4.35
Hasibul Hussain	150.1	8	885	22	40.22	4-56	-	5.89
Manjural Islam	6	0	43	1	43.00	1-43	-	7.16
Minhajul Abedin	71	1	404	9	44.88	2-39	-	5.69
Mohammad Rafique	104.1	6	495	11	45.00	3-55	-	4.75
Neeyamur Rashid	8	1	46	1	46.00	1-46	-	5.75
Aminul Islam	50.4	0	305	5	61.00	3-57	-	6.01
Naimur Rahman	61.4	2	313	5	62.60	2-51	-	5.07
Enamul Hoque	106	0	546	7	78.00	2-46	-	5.15
Akram Khan	19.3	0	138	0	-	-	-	7.07

SHAFIUDDIN AHMED

RHB RFM
Born 1 June 1973

Had taken 10 wickets at 30 runs apiece from the eight one-day international appearances he had made by the start of this World Cup. A fast-medium bowler of ability, Shafi can also hold a bat and is another of Bangladesh's fast-developing cricketers. Made his ut against Zimbabwe at Nairobi during the 1997-98 esident's Cup tournament, and also played in the Silver Jubilee lependence Cup in Dhaka later that winter. Claimed the kets of Saurav Ganguly and Mohammad Azharuddin in one ll during the match against India.

SHAHRIAR HOSSAIN

RHB
Born 1 June 1976

A solid opener who made 95 against Kenya at Dhaka in March, putting on a record first-wicket partnership of 171 with Mehrab Hossain. The two youngsters form an exciting opening pair for this ambitious cricket country. Came into the World Cup with 10 caps, having made his debut against the Kenyans during the 1997-98 President's Cup in Nairobi. He also played against India in the Silver Jubilee Independence Cup. Like so many of his teammates, this World Cup will provide just the sort of top-flight experience he needs at this stage of his career. Was the heaviest run-getter in Bangladesh club cricket last season.

Who else consistently finds the perfect line?

For cricket coverage no-one delivers like The Daily Telegraph.

With an unrivalled line-up of writers and breadth and depth of analysis, it is the last word in cricket.

OFFICIAL
NEWSPAPER OF

World Cup
England 99

The Daily Telegraph
The last word in sport

New Zealand (Group B)

Three times World Cup semi-finalists, and undoubtedly the dark horses of this seventh tournament, New Zealand have an impressive number of fully-fledged all-rounders in their 15-man squad.

Under Stephen Fleming's captaincy the Kiwis have made steady advances during the past two years, both in Test and one-day international cricket. Fleming has worked hard, alongside coach Steve Rixon, the former Australian wicketkeeper, to instil more self-belief and team spirit.

The emergence of talented youngsters like Craig McMillan and Daniel Vettori has helped, too, while Dion Nash's return to fitness and form after a lengthy absence from the international stage has been a big bonus.

Simon Doull, one of the world's most underrated quick bowlers, always leads the attack impressively and all-rounders Chris Cairns, Nathan Astle, Chris Harris, Roger Twose, Gavin Larsen, Nash and McMillan ensure New Zealand are one heck of a combative unit with either bat or ball.

The squad, managed by John Graham, lack an obvious star name in the Richard Hadlee or Martin Crowe category - but Fleming is a left-handed batsman of proven class, and Cairns has the raw ability and power to become one of the world's most-feared all-rounders. Larsen may now be a veteran at 36 but, in more than 100 internationals around the world, his ultra-accurate medium pace has cost well under four runs per over.

Behind the scenes of a resurgent national team, during this past few years, has been a complete overhaul of New Zealand cricket by the country's administrators. Fleming now has the ideal chance to prove that he and his players really have shaken off any previous inferiority complex.

ECB

"I want England to be able to draw on the best players
from all sections of the community. That's why I'm
backing this anti-racism campaign to give every
youngster a chance to enjoy the game to the full."

Brian Lara
West Indies

Alec Stewart
England

Asif Karim
Kenya

Alistair Campbell
Zimbabwe

Steve Waugh
Australia

Mohammad Azharuddin
India

Arjuna Ranatunga
Sri Lanka

George Salmond
Scotland

Stephen Fleming
New Zealand

From playground to Test arena

Aminul Islam
Bangladesh

Hansie Cronje
South Africa

Wasim Akram
Pakistan

SPORTING EQUALS
WORKING FOR RACIAL EQUALITY IN SPORT

STEPHEN FLEMING (C)

LHB
Born 1 April 1973

New Zealand's captain since early 1997, and the youngest-ever when he was appointed mid-way through the short home series with England. Fleming has grown impressively into the job, creating a new spirit of self-belief and underlining his own stature as a batsman of class. Shares the same April Fool's Day birthdate as David Gower, and bats in similarly languid left-handed manner. Made his Test debut in 1993-94, against India at Hamilton, and scored 92. His one-day international debut followed that series but he had to wait until 1996 and 1997, respectively, to reach maiden one-day and Test centuries. Has now made exactly 100 one-day appearances and is perhaps the one truly top-class batsman in a side boasting a string of fine all-rounders.

New Zealand Squad

GEOFF ALLOTT

LHB LFM
Born 24 December 1971

A burly paceman, who hits the pitch hard and has improved his accuracy. Made his Test debut in 1995-96, against Zimbabwe in Hamilton, but had to wait until February 1997 for his one-day international debut, which came against England at Napier. Also made a Test return that spring, having impressed for New Zealand A against the England tourists in Wanganui. Is still relatively inexperienced, though, in both forms of the international game. Can bowl a genuinely quick ball.

NATHAN ASTLE

RHB RM
Born 15 September 1971

New Zealand's most effective one-day batsman, and an unorthodox one. He is a fine improviser and, with his natural timing and power, it makes him a dangerous opponent. Played in the last World Cup, earning himself the man-of-the-match award against England for his 101 from 132 balls, after making his one-day international debut in 1994-95, against the West Indies at Auckland. Started out as a bowler who could bat usefully, but by the time he made his Test debut, against Zimbabwe at Hamilton in 1995-96, it was very much the other way around. His bowling, however, remains effective in the limited-overs game and he has proved to be a useful partnership-breaker at Test level. Had a good season as Nottinghamshire's overseas player in 1997, and that experience of English conditions should be beneficial.

CARL BULFIN

RHB RFM
Born 19 August 1973

A surprise choice for the World Cup squad, but he is quick at times and has a new maturity to add to his raw promise. Used to sport blond dreadlocks, but those have gone these days. Has just moved from Central Districts to Wellington, but has had two good years in domestic cricket - especially in one-day competition. Did not fare too well, though, when given his only one-day international cap to date, against the South Africans earlier this year. One thing is for sure: if he is given a chance he will be up for it.

CHRIS CAIRNS

RHB RFM
Born 16 June 1970

The most explosive batsman in the New Zealand squad, as well as being one of their most potent bowlers. Has the ability to be among the world elite of all-rounders, but so far his career has been something of a disappointment. Injury problems have hampered him as a bowler, but he is the sort of cricketer who can turn a game on its head. After more than a 100 one-day international appearances, the time is right for him to grab centre stage in the biggest tournament of them all. Hits hard and straight, backed by a fine natural technique. Made his Test debut as a 19-year old in 1989-90, against Australia at Perth, and his one-day debut a year later. Was Nottinghamshire's overseas player for several seasons in the mid-90's but, curiously, has yet to bowl a ball for New Zealand in England. Scored the fifth fastest one-day century in history when New Zealand beat India in their fifth one-dayer last winter.

SIMON DOULL
RHB RFM
Born 6 August 1969

Has improved so markedly in the past few years that he is now rated as the best fast bowler New Zealand have had - apart from the great Sir Richard Hadlee. Has certainly taken over from Cairns as the spearhead of the Test and one-day attack, and is currently rated 16th in the Test bowling rankings. His accuracy has also improved, but he still swings the ball both ways and in English conditions should get seam movement too. Actually made both his Test and one-day international debuts as long ago as 1992-93, against Zimbabwe in Bulawayo. It was not until the second half of the decade, however, that he began to win a regular place.

CHRIS HARRIS
LHB RM/LB
Born 20 November 1969

One of the world's leading one-day specialists - a hard-hitting batsman, an inventive bowler of leg-cutters or leg-breaks off a short run, and a quite brilliant fielder. Harris is best remembered for his heroic 130 against Australia in the 1996 World Cup quarter-final, and is something of a cult figure in New Zealand. Perhaps the wider stage awaits him again. Has hardly figured at Test level, but had appeared in 127 one-day internationals before the start of this World Cup. His one-day debut came back in 1990-91, in a World Series international against Australia at Sydney.

MATTHEW HART
LHB SLA
Born 16 May 1972

Has won 14 Test caps but had only 11 limited-overs appearances behind him at the start of this World Cup. His international career has been in decline since the arrival of Daniel Vettori to bowl classic left-arm spin from early 1997, but his call-up for this tournament - though very much out of the blue - proves he still has much to play for. Is a better batsman than Vettori, despite the youngster's improvement in that department, and has had a good all-round domestic season for Northern Districts. Bowls a tighter line and length than Vettori, and his one-day best figures of 5-22 against the West Indies in 1994 are also New Zealand's best. Is a good enough spinner to have won a Test for the Kiwis, also in 1994 and against South Africa.

MATTHEW HORNE
RHB
Born 5 February 1970

Made both his Test and one-day international debuts in early 1997, and has since developed into a stylish and dependable opening batsman. His highest Test score is 157, made against Zimbabwe at Auckland in February 1998, and he is particularly strong off the front foot. Might, however, be exposed outside his off stump against the moving ball. Good enough to have completed 1000 Test run in his 14th match and won a place in this World Cup for his solidity rather than his record in one-day internationals, which was moderate at best before the tournament began.

GAVIN LARSEN
RHB RM
Born 27 September 1962

Perhaps the most unsung 'star' of limited-overs international cricket during the past decade. Larsen took 107 wickets in 113 one-day appearances for New Zealand leading up to this World Cup, but even more significantly had conceded just 3.79 runs per over. In all conditions, and in every corner of the world, Larsen's accuracy has not let his line down - despite the military medium pace of his bowling. On slow, seaming pitches he has often proved almost impossible to get away, and had made 55 one-day appearances before winning the first of his eight Test caps in 1994. His limited-overs international debut came in 1989-90, against India at Dunedin.

CRAIG MCMILLAN
RHB RM
Born 13 September 1976

Very much the rising star of New Zealand cricket, a highly-talented and attractive batsman with a wide range of strokes, and a combative medium-pacer with the ball. His firs one-day international cap came in the 1996-97 Independence Cup tournament, against Sri Lanka at Hyderabad, but a first Test appearance did not arrive until a year later, against Australia in Brisbane. Perhaps the New Zealand selectors held him back a little too much: after 11 Tests he averages 48.94 and is currently ranked fifth best batsman in the world. Had played 39 one-day internationals before this World Cup and is ready to take on the best.

WASIM AKRAM (C)

LHB LF
Born 3 June 1966

Many would say Wasim is the best left-arm pace bowler world cricket has seen, and he is certainly still young enough, fit enough and quick enough to challenge for Kapil Dev's Test record of 434 wickets. He has already been a World Cup final match-winner, his 33 not out from [?]t 18 balls and the wickets of Botham, Lamb and Lewis [swi]nging the 1992 final Pakistan's way. Holds the record for the [nu]mber of one-day international wickets and always seems to rise [to] the big occasion, like any true great. Generates huge pace and [mo]vement from a short run, fast arm and fine wrist action. His [ba]tting has generally been disappointing, but his ability is such [tha]t he hit a maiden Test hundred against Australia almost 10 [yea]rs ago and, in 1996-97, smashed 257 not out against [Zi]mbabwe - from the number eight position.

Pakistan Squad

World Cup

ABDUR RAZZAQ

RHB RM
Born 2 Decmber 1979

Still only 18, Abdur is regarded as an all-rounder of great promise. He is one of the chief successes of Pakistan's burgeoning under 19 policy, having toured both New Zealand and the West Indies at that level. He also toured England in 1997 with Pakistan A and is an [ex]cellent outfielder. Pakistan's selectors have also been quick to [gi]ve Abdur a taste of the highest level. At the start of this World [Cu]p he had played 14 one-day internationals, with a top score of [?] not out and best bowling figures of 3-48.

AZHAR MAHMOOD

RHB RFM
Born 28 February 1975

A fine all-rounder who has quickly established himself in the Pakistan squad. His upright, clean-hitting batsmanship brought him three hundreds in the short 1997-98 series against South Africa, and his purposeful fast-medium either provides ideal support to the pace of Wasim, Waqar and now Shoaib in the Test team or the perfect balance to the one-day international side. His bowling could become an even stronger suit than his lower middle-order batting in English conditions, which should suit his style. First came to prominence with some lusty hitting and competitive bowling displays against the touring England A team in late 1995.

IJAZ AHMED

RHB
Born 20 September 1968

The great survivor of the Pakistan top order, Ijaz played his first Test - against India in Madras - as long ago as 1986-87, when he was 18. In and out of the side for more than a decade, he finally passed the 50-Test mark in December 1998 and, in recent times, has at last become a [pe]rmanent fixture - usually batting at number three. A fine [fie]lder, with an unerringly accurate throw, he also bowled a [sig]nificant number of overs with his left-arm medium pace in the [19]92 World Cup triumph. But nowadays he is chosen exclusively [fo]r his consistency with the bat and the ability to play a genuinely [de]structive innings when the mood takes him.In the 1997-98 [W]ills Challenge Series, for instance, India's attack were thrashed [fo]r an 84-ball 139 at Lahore - Ijaz's remarkable hitting bringing [hi]m no less than nine sixes and 10 fours.

INZAMAM-UL-HAQ

RHB
Born 3 March 1970

The hulking Haq made a dramatic entry into international cricket during the 1992 World Cup, rescuing Pakistan from a position of near-despair in their semi-final against New Zealand at Auckland. The young unknown strode in to strike a blistering 60 from just 37 balls to swing the match back Pakistan's way. In the final, against England, he then hit 42 off 35 balls to help Pakistan post a total that proved just out of reach for Graham Gooch's side. Opinion is divided in Pakistan as to whether Inzamam has so far fulfilled his awesome talent: his figures proclaim him as his country's best and most consistent middle-order batsman since the heyday of Javed Miandad, but his regular dismissals run-out and his tendency to play a lazy shot, all hint towards a lack of total concentration to the job in hand.

MOIN KHAN

RHB WK
Born 23 September 1971

A safe pair of hands behind the stumps, an influential member of the dressing room, a never-say-die character, and a lower middle-order batsman who always seems to save his best for when Pakistan are in a tight spot. Moin is now undisputedly Pakistan's number one keeper-batsman, although the currently out-of-favour Rashid Latif has been preferred in several series in recent years. He made his Test debut against the West Indies in 1990-91 and soon established himself as the natural successor to Salim Yousuf. He played in the 1992 World Cup final win against England, having contributed a swashbuckling 20 not out from only 11 balls to help wrap up the thrilling semi-final victory against New Zealand.

MUSHTAQ AHMED

RHB LB
Born 28 June 1970

A leg-spinner of world-class, who 1995-96 challenged even the great Shane Warne for the mantle of world's number one slow bowler. Between November 1995 and August 1996 he took 45 wickets in six Tests, baffling first Australia's batsmen and then England's with rich bag of tricks. He has won many admirers around the world for his bouncy style, and evident relish of his art, and has been an immensely popular member of Somerset's team since he joined the county in 1993. Took 3-41 in the 1992 World Cup final, trapping Graeme Hick lbw with a classic googly and also snapping up the prized wicket of Graham Gooch as Pakistan swept to their most famous one-day victory. His knowledge of English conditions could be important to Pakistan's World Cup hopes this time.

SAEED ANWAR

LHB
Born 6 September 1968

A class act at the top of the Pakistan order, as his epic match-winning 188 not out in the Asian Test Championship victory over India at Calcutta in February proved. Saeed has the concentration and technical solidity to play a long, defensive innings - and also the range of strokeplay and controlled aggression to go straight on to the attack in a limited-overs match. He averages above 40 in both Test and one-day international cricket, the benchmark of the very good. Scored 176 against England at The Oval during Pakistan's 1996 tour, ending the trip with a total of 1,224 first-class runs at an average of 68. Has 15 one-day international hundreds to his name, including the highest individual score made in a limited-overs international - the 194 struck off India in the 1997-98 Independence Cup at Madras. One of Pakistan's key men at this World Cup.

SALIM MALIK

RHB
Born 16 April 1963

One of the most consistent and underrated batsmen in recent Test history. This World Cup could be a glorious final chapter in a Pakistan career stretching back to 1981-82, the winter in which he made both his Test and one-day international debuts. Made a dramatic comeback to top-flight cricket last winter, winning his 100th Test cap in December 1998. He is also closing in on a 300th one-day international appearance. A determined player, and at his best a sweet timer of the cricket ball. Played county cricket for Essex.

SAQLAIN MUSHTAQ

RHB OB
Born 27 November 1976

Rivals controversial Sri Lankan Muttiah Muralitharan as the world's best off-spinner, and is fiendishly difficult to attack in one-day cricket. Took a wicket with his seventh ball in Test cricket against Sri Lanka at Peshawar in 1995-96, and is the master of the off-spinner's 'mystery ball' - the one which somehow spins away from the right-hander. A product of backstreet cricket in his home city of Lahore, he is a mature cricketer beyond his years and has an excellent temperament for both Test and one-day cricket. His effectiveness in both forms of the game can be seen from the fact that, in the past three years, he has taken more wickets than any of his equally world-class teammates. Surprisingly, though he was then still very young, he played just one game during the 1996 World Cup. Has become an instant favourite at Surrey, whom he joined in 1997.

SHAHID AFRIDI

RHB LB
Born 1 March 1980

A massive talent, with more than 70 one-day international appearances to his name - and he is still only 19! Created a sensation as a 16-year old back in the 1996-97 Kenya Centenary tournament in Nairobi when, called up as a last-minute replacement for the injured Mushtaq Ahmed, he was sent in first to 'pinch-hit' by his skipper Saeed Anwar and responded by smashing the Sri Lankan attack for an astonishing 37-ball international debut century! Since then he has been regularly used as a one-day opener, but much of the past two years has been spent gathering experience to go with the talent. Bowls fast leg-breaks to give the already potent Pakistan attack a further option, and is a steady fielder. Made his Test debut against Australia, at Karachi, only last October and is still relatively green at that level.

SHOAIB AKHTAR

RHB RF
Born 13 August 1975

At 23 the Rawalpindi Express has the world at his feet. He was named Man of the Tournament at the Coca-Cola Cup in Sharjah in April, winning a new car, and is so highly-rated by Pakistan that he kept Waqar Younis out of the team. On his first overseas tour, to South Africa in 97-98, he was timed as being faster than both Waqar and lan Donald. He shocked India's classy top order with his pace lier this year, including Sachin Tendulkar, and is probably the rld's fastest bowler at the present time. Made his Test debut inst the West Indies in 1997-98, and his first one-day ernational against Zimbabwe later that same winter. Pace is sed on strong physique, aggressive run-up and smooth but olosive action. English counties could be queueing for his nature if he impresses in this World Cup.

WAJAHATULLAH WASTI

RHB OB
Born 11 November 1974

Made 31 in only his second one-day international, against England in Sharjah in April, but it is in Test cricket that opening batsman Wasti has so far made the biggest waves. He made his Test debut against India in Calcutta in the Asian Test Championship earlier this year.

en, in Pakistan's next Test, against Sri Lanka in Lahore, he ored a hundred in both innings. He also represented Pakistan the 1998 Commonwealth Games. From Peshawar on the old orth-West Frontier, he plays for Allied Bank.

WAQAR YOUNIS

RHB RF
Born 16 November 1971

One of the most destructive bowlers in the history of the game, as his Test record (277 wickets from 57 Tests at 21.96) amply demonstrates. Waqar simply exploded on to the world scene in 1989-90 after, reportedly, Imran Khan called him into the Pakistan squad after seeing m bowl in a televised club game. Waqar was a day short of his 3th birthday when he made his Test debut, against India at arachi, and in his first 11 Tests he took 55 wickets, with five uls of five wickets or more. A huge number of Waqar's victims ve been taken lbw, or bowled - testimony to his accuracy and so to rapid pace allied to murderously late swing. On the county cuit, following his deeds with both Surrey and Glamorgan, hom he helped to the championship title in 1997, any batsman ho gets smashed painfully on the toes by an inswinging yorker now referred to as being 'Waqar-ed'.

Pakistan Squad One-Day Career Averages
Based on all matches played up to 30/04/1999

BATTING AND FIELDING

NAME	M	I	NO	RUNS	HS	AVGE	100	50	CT	ST
Yousuf Youhana	20	16	2	576	100	41.14	1	5	7	-
Saeed Anwar	170	168	14	6172	194	40.07	15	30	32	-
Inzamam-ul-Haq	182	172	23	5868	137˙	39.38	6	41	47	-
Salim Malik	279	252	38	7152	102	33.42	5	47	80	-
Ijaz Ahmed	226	209	28	5986	139˙	33.07	10	32	83	-
Wajahatullah Wasti	3	3	0	86	37	28.66	-	-	1	-
Shahid Afridi	82	79	2	1912	109	24.83	2	10	29	-
Moin Khan	129	107	28	1895	69˙	23.98	-	6	116	45
Shoaib Akhtar	16	7	4	52	36	17.33	-	-	3	-
Azhar Mahmood	60	45	10	606	65˙	17.31	-	2	19	-
Wasim Akram	265	208	37	2676	86	15.64	-	6	70	-
Saqlain Mushtaq	98	56	19	469	30˙	12.67	-	-	26	-
Abdur Razzaq	14	11	2	105	46˙	11.66	-	-	1	-
Waqar Younis	172	85	31	538	37	9.96	-	-	19	-
Mushtaq Ahmed	130	69	31	343	26	9.02	-	-	28	-

BOWLING

NAME	O	M	R	W	AVGE	BEST	5W	ECON
Wajahatullah Wasti	5.1	0	40	3	13.33	3-36	-	7.74
Saqlain Mushtaq	856.1	42	3633	187	19.42	5-29	4	4.24
Shoaib Akhtar	127	15	526	27	19.48	4-37	-	4.14
Waqar Younis	1426.5	95	6545	283	23.12	6-26	9	4.58
Wasim Akram	2266.5	167	8716	371	23.49	5-15	5	3.84
Inzamam-ul-Haq	6.4	0	52	2	26.00	1-4	-	7.80
Abdur Razzaq	88.4	2	462	14	33.00	3-48	-	5.21
Salim Malik	584	10	2959	89	33.24	5-35	1	5.06
Mushtaq Ahmed	1120.3	43	4842	144	33.62	5-36	1	4.32
Saeed Anwar	36.2	3	176	5	35.20	2-9	-	4.84
Azhar Mahmood	449.3	30	2018	53	38.07	5-38	1	4.48
Shahid Afridi	572	14	2713	53	51.18	3-33	-	4.74
Ijaz Ahmed	105.2	1	474	5	94.80	2-31	-	4.50

YOUSUF YOUHANA

LHB
Born 27 August 1974

A compact, technically-proficient middle-order batsman who has made a fine start to his international career over the past 18 months. Can play either a defensive or attacking role and averaged more than 40 in his first dozen Test innings after making his debut against South Africa at Durban in 1997-98. First came to the notice of the wider public when Pakistan's selectors picked him in their A team for a couple of pre-Sharjah tournament warm-up matches against England in Lahore in December 1997. Youhana, one of the few Christians to represent Pakistan, made his one-day international debut in 1997-98, against Zimbabwe in Harare and - an instant success again - after more than a dozen appearances he averaged 50.

www.easports.com

ROW Z
TAKE COVER

Cricket
World Cup

EA SPORTS

if it's in the game
it's in the game

PC
CD

The only official computer game of the Cricket World Cup 1999.

Scotland (Group B)

Bravehearts, indeed, will be needed in a group headed by Australia, ...kistan and the West Indies – ...t Scottish cricket has already ...en given a massive boost by ...e very act of qualifying for this ...st World Cup appearance.

Long-serving captain George ...lmond called the 1997 ICC Trophy ...ird-place play-off win against Ireland – ...e result which clinched their World Cup ...ow – "the proudest moment of my ...reer". And so it was, even for a player ...th more than 100 Scotland appearances ... his name.

Now, in 1999, and boosted by the ...ailability of highly-promising ...orkshire all-rounder Gavin ...amilton, the Scots face the ...ost crucial year of their ...ng cricket history.

Good performances ...ainst the game's top ...ations – especially in their ...vo home fixtures – will go a ...ng way towards clinching for ...cotland the official one-day ...ternational status which the ...CC granted Bangladesh and ...enya 18 months ago, and ...hich has already done so ...uch to promote the growth of cricket ...ill further in those two countries.

Scottish cricket has been strengthened ...onsiderably in recent years, and not ...erely through their qualification for this ...World Cup. A new national league has ...een formed for this season, and a policy of attracting good-class touring teams has already been established.

Bangladesh and a strong Australia A side toured Scotland last summer, and proof that Salmond's team was responding to the stiffer competition and increased professionalism came with a historic first NatWest Trophy victory, against Worcestershire at Edinburgh.

One man who has played a leading role in Scotland's advance is their coach Jim Love, the former Yorkshire batsman. He was appointed in October 1992 and, after Scotland won their independence from England in 1994 by being made an associate member of the ICC – and thus a cricket nation in their own right – Love set about building the professional approach to both practice and match-play that is essential for improvement.

Hamilton and John Blain, of Northamptonshire, are the only two full-time professionals but the rest of the squad are just as committed. Scotland prepared for the World Cup by undertaking an 11-day training trip to Sharjah in mid-April, with former Kent and England paceman Graham Dilley going with them as bowling coach. The World Cup squad is managed by R G Hill.

GEORGE SALMOND (C)

RHB
Born 1 December 1969

The man leading Scotland in their biggest cricket challenge has been groomed for the job all his playing life. A former captain of Scotland at under 16, under 19 and B level, Salmond took over command of the senior side in 1995 and has since led with panache and style. A sound ...ctician, he is also capable of playing inspirational innings with ...e bat. Now vastly experienced, with more than 100 Scotland ...ppearances to his name, he is a quick-footed middle-order ...tsman who once made 181 against Ireland. A primary school ...acher in Edinburgh, he plays for the Grange club - whose ...aeburn Place ground will stage the Scots' two big home ...atches in this World Cup, against Bangladesh and New ...ealand.

Scotland Squad

World Cup

MIKE ALLINGHAM

RHB RM
Born 6 January 1965

A genuine all-rounder who hails from the Highlands, and once a promising rugby player who played for Scotland B at scrum-half before a serious knee injury halted his progress. He is now a schoolmaster at Fettes College in Edinburgh - Tony Blair's old school. First played ...r Scotland in 1991, and is a handy man to have around both in ...e middle-order and with the ball.

JOHN BLAIN

RHB RFM
Born 4 January 1979

One of the most promising cricketers to have emerged north of the border, Blain became the youngest player to represent Scotland when he made his debut three years ago against Ireland, aged 17. Has been on Northamptonshire's books since 1997, and during that summer took 5-24 against Derbyshire on his Sunday League debut. Improving with the bat, he is also a fine fielder and a genuine all-round prospect.

JAMES BRINKLEY

RHB RFM
Born 13 March 1974

A key new ball bowler for the Scots, Brinkley has the advantage of county experience with both Worcestershire and Essex - as well as spells with Matebeleland in Zimbabwe and a grounding in Australia, where he grew up. Took 6-98 for Worcestershire against Surrey, at The ...val, on his county championship debut in 1994. Born in ...elensburgh, he made his first appearance for Scotland in the ...998 Benson and Hedges Cup competition.

ASIM BUTT

RHB LFM
Born 2 May 1968

Made his Scotland debut on his 30th birthday last summer, winning the man-of-the-match award for his 3-42 in a three-wicket defeat by Yorkshire at Linlithgow in the Benson and Hedges Cup. Born in Lahore, for whom he played a few first-class games before emigration, it had taken Butt four years of protracted negotiations to be granted qualification for his adopted country. A left-arm seamer who hits the pitch hard, and has that necessary extra yard of pace to hurry the best batsmen. Late order slogger.

ALEC DAVIES

RHB WK
Born 18 April 1962

Like Butt, born in Pakistan, but only because his father was a diplomat who happened to be posted there at the time. Was on Surrey's books in the mid-80's and played one first-class match for them, against the touring Sri Lankans, in 1985. A stylish batsman in the lower middle-order, he made his Scotland debut in 1993 and has been the regular, first-choice keeper since 1995. Works as a sports development officer for the West Lothian Council and is a fit 37, as befits someone with physical education qualifications.

NICK DYER

RHB OB
Born 10 June 1969

Bowled with skill and great econor during last summer's Benson and Hedges Cup campaign, and is an off-spinner with good control and nice loop. A teacher, he plays Susse League cricket with Chichester, an is also a fine fielder. Made his first-class debut in 1997, playing for Scotland against Ireland. Has no pretensions with the bat, but i that Ireland match played out the last 15 balls of the match to earn the Scots a draw.

GAVIN HAMILTON

RHB RFM
Born 16 September 1974

Scotland's key all-rounder, but almost played for England in this World Cup. Hamilton was named in England's provisional World Cup squad after a brilliant 1998 county season for Yorkshire, in which he took 56 championship wickets at 20.41 and scored 572 runs at an average of 33.64. A change in ICC rules, however, allowed Hamilton to continue playing for his native land (an associate member) even though he has understandable ambitions to play full Test cricket. Once he had missed out this time with England, he was overjoyed to be able to resume his Scotland career without it affecting his England qualification. The World Cup is an ideal next stage for his development.

BRUCE PATTERSON

RHB
Born 29 January 1965

With initials like BMW you woulc expect a bit of style, and this 34-ye old opener from Ayr is a tall, elegan strokemaker who hopes to win his 100th Scottish cap during this World Cup. Has formed an effectiv and enduring opening partnership with Iain Philip down the years, an marked his Scotland debut in 1988 with a century against Ireland. Made 70 against Allan Border's 1989 Australians, but had to fight his way back into the side after being omitted from the squad taken to contest the 1997 ICC Trophy in Malaysia. Returned, however, with a century against Denmark and was an ever-present in Scotland's four Benson and Hedges Cup and tw NatWest Trophy matches last summer.

IAIN PHILIP

RHB
Born 9 June 1958

Even at almost 41 Philip is an important figure in Scotland's first World Cup campaign. A prolific batsman, he has scored nearly 5,000 runs for his country since making his first appearance back in 1986. Born in Stenhousemuir, his family moved to Australia when he was 11, and he still winters in Perth every year. With his Aussie background, he was particularly delighted to score a hundred against the touring Australia A team last summer - an attack which included Jason Gillespie and Brendon Julian. He is Scotland's most-capped player, and holds the record individual score (234 v MCC in 1991) as well as the records for most runs and most hundreds. An elegant timer of the ball, he is especially strong through the covers. Has also kept wicket for Scotland, and serves as Alec Davies' understudy in this World Cup.

KEITH SHERIDAN

RHB SLA
Born 26 March 1971

A skiddy slow left-arm spinner whc included the scalps of both Steve ar Mark Waugh in a haul of 5-65 against the 1997 Australians, and who picked up 4-34 in the vital IC Trophy third-place play-off victory against Ireland later that year. A civ engineer by trade, he was one of Scotland's youngest players when he made his debut in 1989. A product of the coaching scheme run by former Scotland stalwart Omar Henry.

MIKE SMITH

RHB RM
Born 30 March 1966

Potentially Scotland's best batsman, and certainly the most naturally-gifted. But Smith has suffered from inconsistency, even being dropped by the selectors from 1990 to 1994. Scored 79 on his debut in 1987, against Ireland. Typically, was Scotland's top scorer in the match at got them to the World Cup - the play-off encounter with eland in the 1997 ICC Trophy - but before that had been left at of the side again. A sales representative, and the son of a actor, he plays for Aberdeenshire and has also been a good-class gby player.

IAN STANGER

RHB RM
Born 5 October 1971

Had a season on Leicestershire's books in 1994, after being voted Scotland's young cricketer of the year for both 1992 and 1993. Made his Scotland debut in 1992, but a highly-promising early career as a genuine all-rounder was interrupted by a string of injuries. Captained cotland at both under 16 and under 19 levels and has spent ecent winters either in South Africa or Australia. In recent easons has been working hard to further develop his batting, which is now his stronger suit. Is still a useful change bowler with is seamers, but enjoyed more success with the bat against australia A last summer.

PETER STEINDL

RHB RM
Born 14 June 1970

An Australian from Queensland who came to Scotland in 1991 to play as the Cupar Club's professional, married a Scottish girl and never went back. Now has two daughters and went into this World Cup with 23 Scotland caps to his name following his qualification to play for is adopted country. Is a cricket development officer for the cottish Cricket Union and has put in some steady performances with the ball and as a late-order batsman.

GREIG WILLIAMSON

RHB RM
Born 20 Decemeber 1968

A competitive all-rounder and a superb fielder who should be at the peak of his powers. He was first picked for Scotland at the tender age of 20, in 1989, but then did not play again until 1993. Took 3-68 and hit 57 against the 1995 West Indians. An aggressive batsman in the middle-order, and a still-improving seamer. A qualified accountant and lawyer, he works as a solicitor in Glasgow and was given the Christian names John Greig after the former Rangers and Scotland football captain. A member of the Clydesdale club.

West Indies (Group B)

West Indian cricket had an almost biblical experience during the winter; in South Africa, where they were thrashed 5-0 in the Test series and 6-1 in the one-dayers, they looked dead and buried as a world power. But, inspired by Brian Lara's majestic batting and the fast bowling old firm of Ambrose and Walsh, they bounced back in the Caribbean to hold Australia 2-2 in one of the most memorable Test series of all time.

That triumvirate looks like holding the key to their World Cup performance, too, although Shivnarine Chanderpaul is a proven and accomplished limited-overs player.

A glance at the management team of Clive Lloyd and Malcolm Marshall, however, is all you need to remind yourself of the true power and glory of past West Indies teams.

Manager Lloyd, of course, led West Indies to their World Cup triumphs of 1975 and 1979 - besides hitting the first, and perhaps, best century of the three so far made in a World Cup final. Marshall, now coach, was in the 1983 World Cup final side beaten so surprisingly by India at Lord's.

Lloyd's 102, from 85 balls, spearheaded the 1975 final win against Australia. Four years later Lloyd could sit back and admire Viv Richards' magnificent unbeaten 138, Collis King's explosive 66-ball 86, and the fearsome Joel Garner's dismissive 5-38 as England were slain by 92 runs in the 1979 final.

Over-confidence, facing a moderate Indian total of 183, has been blamed for the 1983 final failure. Certainly, it is hard to conceive of a side boasting an attack of Marshall, Andy Roberts, Garner and Michael Holding experiencing defeat.

But Lloyd was hampered by a leg injury and Richards, after hammering 33 from just 28 balls, fell to a nerveless running catch by Indian captain Kapil Dev. India's battery of seamers increased the pressure in helpful conditions, and yet another great sporting occasion threw up an underdog victor.

In 1987 and 1992 the West Indies failed to qualify from the group stages, and some said the more severe one-day restrictions on bowlers, regarding what was classified as either a no-ball or wide, was putting a stranglehold on the out-and-out quickie's effectiveness in the limited-overs game.

Nevertheless, under Richie Richardson, the West Indies reached the semi-finals at the 1996 tournament before falling to Australia in a remarkable contest in Chandigarh. Needing just 43 from the last nine overs after Chanderpaul's 80 and Lara's 45, and with eight wickets still in hand, the West Indies were undermined by Shane Warne (4-36) and bowled out for 202. Richardson was left stranded on 49 not out, his team stunned by a five-run defeat. •

BRIAN LARA (C)

LHB
Born 2 May 1969

Who is the best batsman in the world today? Lara, or Sachin Tendulkar? That question may not be answered until both have finished their international careers, but their rivalry for the number one ranking may inspire them to even greater heights of performance during this World Cup and beyond. Lara has already played some of the greatest innings of all time, two of them in successive Tests this spring when he hit the Australian bowlers for a double century to help win the Trinidad Test and then a quite sensational unbeaten 153 to lead the West Indies to glory at Barbados in one of the great finishes. Between April and June 1994 he claimed both the highest Test score, 375 against England in Antigua, and the highest first-class score in history - an awesome 501 not out for Warwickshire against Durham at Edgbaston. Without doubt the most exciting batsman to watch in the modern game.

West Indies Squad

World Cup

JIMMY ADAMS

LHB SLA
Born 9 January 1968

Adams is the Mr Reliable of the West Indies team, although he is very much in the middle of an international comeback following a slump in fortunes in recent times. That in itself was a surprise, given the impact Adams first made when he strode on to the Test stage in 1991-92. For a long time in the mid-90's he was ranked number one in the world, but then he suffered through a loss of form and fitness. Missed last winter's disastrous tour of South Africa when he severed a tendon in his hand in an accident with a breadknife during the outward flight. But he bounced back in style against Australia, giving magnificent support to Brian Lara both on and off the field. Sometimes keeps wicket in one-day internationals; otherwise he is a useful part-time slow left armer.

CURTLY AMBROSE

LHB RFM
Born 21 September 1963

The giant Antiguan has been the West Indies' spearhead since the retirement of Malcolm Marshall and deserves to be ranked in the highest bracket of other Caribbean quicks like Hall, Roberts, Holding and Garner. Perhaps, at his best, he was the nearest thing there has been to Garner, especially with his great height and the ability to emulate the fearsome Barbadian's lethal yorkers. Ambrose, who was more interested in basketball than cricket as a teenager, burst on to the scene in the West Indies by taking 35 wickets at just 15 runs apiece in his debut season of 1987-88. A first Test cap, against Pakistan in Guyana, followed in April 1988, and he was soon terrorising the world's best batsmen. He once took five wickets for one run against Australia in Perth. Now, in his mid-30's, he has lost a couple of yards of pace but is still very difficult to hit.

KEITH ARTHURTON

LHB SLA
Born 21 February 1965

Never a Test regular, Arthurton's main service to West Indian cricket is illustrated by his 100-plus one-day international caps. At 34 he is in the twilight of his career, but he does not look like a senior citizen in the field. Arthurton remains one of the quickest ground fielders in the world, and his left-arm spinners are often used in the limited-overs arena. A dangerous batsman, who can score very quickly when the force is with him, he is a proud representative of the tiny Leeward island of Nevis - and only its third Test cricketer. Is taking part in his third World Cup.

HENDERSON BRYAN

RHB RFM
Born 21 March 1970

Known as 'Hendy', he has come late to international cricket but seems immediately in tune with its demands - and certainly in the limited-overs game. An instant hit in the recent series against Australia, taking 4-24 on his debut, he struck a blow for the previously forgotten generation of twentysomething Caribbean cricketers with his performances with bat and ball. A stalwart of Barbados, whom he helped to domestic honours last winter, he is a strong-looking bowler of brisk medium pace and a hard-hitting batsman in the best West Indian tradition. Also has a good arm in the field.

SHERWIN CAMPBELL

RHB
Born 1 November 1970

A dependable opener, who has had experience of county cricket with Durham. Enjoyed a comeback series against Australia in March and April, and was then retained for the one-day series which followed. Had lost his place when the West Indies selectors opted for an opening ombination of Philo Wallace and Clayton Lambert. Made his rst-class debut for Barbados at 20, and is a former captain of Vest Indies Youth. Scored half-centuries in each of his first two ests, against New Zealand, and averages almost 40 in the five-ay game. His one-day performances have been sketchier, but yone with a Test double hundred to his name (Campbell hit)8 against New Zealand in 1995-96) must be worth persevering ith. Also has two Test centuries against Australia.

SHIVNARINE CHANDERPAUL

LHB LB
Born 18 August 1974

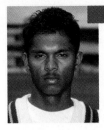

A middle-order batsman of genuine Test class, Chanderpaul has also enjoyed significant success in one-day internationals as an opener. Small in stature, and effective rather than pleasing in style, he became the first teenager to play Test cricket for the West Indies for more than 20 years when selected against England in his native Guyana in early 1994. Four half-centuries in his first four Tests amply demonstrated his determination to succeed as well as his powers of concentration and - four years on - he won the man-of-the-match award for hitting a century against England in Georgetown. Made his one-day debut in 1994-95 and is a brilliant fielder in any position.

MERVYN DILLON

RHB RFM
Born 5 June 1974

Rated as one of the most promising of the new generation of West Indian fast bowlers, but also worryingly prone to injury. Took five Pakistan wickets in Karachi in 1997, however, and in last year's Wills Cup semi-final he demolished India's much-vaunted batting line-up. efore this World Cup, though, he had played in just 12 one-day nternationals and has not managed to establish himself on the est stage. Played his first Test against India in 1996-97. Moves he ball predominantly into the right hander, and may have to arn how to straighten it consistently off the pitch if he is to evelop into a top-class quick.

RIDLEY JACOBS

LHB WK
Born 26 November 1967

A late developer, but now one of the most dependable members of the West Indies squad. Was one of the few successes of the disastrous tour of South Africa last winter, in which he was voted man of the series for the West Indies. Made his one-day international debut against England on April 1 last year, but quickly showed he was nobody's fool either with the keeper's gloves or with bat in hand. The Antiguan has been a permanent fixture ever since, apart from the odd one-day game in which Jimmy Adams takes over the gloves. Left-handed, a real battler with the bat in the middle-order and has been used as a pinch-hitter at the head of the order.

REON KING

RHB RF
Born 6 October 1975

Only made his Guyana debut in 1996, so has risen quickly through the ranks. Made his one-day debut in last autumn's Mini World Cup in Bangladesh and is genuinely quick. Needs to improve his fitness to overcome knee problems, but is young enough to learn from this Vorld Cup experience. The West Indies are looking at such as King to replace, eventually, their veteran strike force of Ambrose nd Walsh. Swings the new ball appreciably, and has been vorking on his control and accuracy. A good, rhythmical run-up.

NEHEMIAH PERRY

RHB OB
Born 16 June 1968

Consistent and dependable Jamaican off-spinner who suddenly, against the Australians this spring, found himself starting a Test career at the age of 30. He responded brilliantly, showing all his experience by taking a second innings 5-70 on his debut as the West Indies fought back to win the Second Test on his home island. Held his place for the rest of that magnificent series and, as a bonus, won selection for the World Cup too. Previously, the nearest he had come to international recognition was selection for West Indies A against England A in 1992 and a non-playing squad member in Sharjah in late 1996.

RICARDO POWELL

RHB OB
Born 15 December 1978

The late replacement for Carl Hooper, who announced his retirement from international cricket in mid-April after initially being included in the World Cup Squad. Powell, a Jamaican, is like Hooper, an off-spinning all-rounder. He made his first class debut only last year but, during the winter, scored a hundred-and-half century in a game against Barbados and also represented both a West Indies Board XI and the West Indies A team against the touring Australians.

PHIL SIMMONS

RHB RM
Born 18 April 1963

A veteran all-rounder who made his one-day international debut against Pakistan in Lahore during the 1987 World Cup, and is now approaching 150 limited-overs caps. But he has never been able to hold down such a regular place in the West Indies' Test team. Has enjoyed some of the best moments of his professional career with Leicestershire, whom he has helped to county championship titles in 1996 and 1998. Made 261, too, on his debut for the county back in 1994, so no wonder he is much-loved at Grace Road. In 1988, on his first tour of England, he needed a life-saving operation after being struck a sickening blow on the head when batting against Gloucestershire's David Lawrence. A powerful striker of the ball, as befits his size, and still a useful medium pacer.

West Indies Squad One-Day Career Averages
Based on all matches played up to 30/04/1999

BATTING AND FIELDING

NAME	M	I	NO	RUNS	HS	AVGE	100	50	CT	ST
B.C.Lara	141	139	14	5628	169	45.02	12	37	64	-
R.D.King	12	8	7	38	12*	38.00	-	-	2	-
S.Chanderpaul	66	62	4	2018	150	34.79	2	12	20	-
S.C.Williams	53	52	5	1569	105*	33.38	1	12	13	-
J.C.Adams	81	64	21	1307	82	30.39	-	8	54	5
P.V.Simmons	138	135	11	3662	122	29.53	5	18	53	-
K.L.T.Arthurton	104	92	20	1898	84	26.36	-	9	27	-
S.L.Campbell	45	45	0	1153	86	25.62	-	6	10	-
N.O.Perry	5	3	2	24	9	24.00	-	-	-	-
M.Dillon	16	5	4	21	13*	21.00	-	-	1	-
R.D.Jacobs	23	18	3	287	68	19.13	-	2	25	6
C.E.L.Ambrose	161	88	34	615	31*	11.38	-	-	43	-
C.A.Walsh	188	70	29	295	30	7.19	-	-	27	-
H.R.Bryan	6	3	0	12	6	4.00	-	-	1	-

BOWLING

NAME	O	M	R	W	AVGE	BEST	5W	ECON
B.C.Lara	5	0	34	2	17.00	2-5	-	6.80
C.E.L.Ambrose	1430.5	175	5117	213	24.02	5-17	4	3.57
M.Dillon	136.2	11	644	24	26.83	4-20	-	4.72
N.O.Perry	34.2	1	136	5	27.20	3-45	-	3.96
K.L.T.Arthurton	229.4	4	1150	42	27.38	4-31	-	5.00
S.C.Williams	4	0	30	1	30.00	1-30	-	7.50
R.D.King	111	7	482	16	30.12	3-40	-	4.34
J.C.Adams	139	7	668	22	30.36	5-37	1	4.80
C.A.Walsh	1652.4	159	6418	206	31.15	5-1	1	3.88
P.V.Simmons	607.4	33	2740	78	35.12	4-3	-	4.50
S.Chanderpaul	89.4	0	469	12	39.08	3-18	-	5.23
H.R.Bryan	50	3	236	5	47.20	4-24	-	4.72

COURTNEY WALSH

RHB RF
Born 30 October 1962

Like Ol' Man River, he just keeps rollin' along. The giant, genial Jamaican first toured England with the West Indies in 1984, breaking into the Test team later that year and having made his first-class debut as long ago as 1981. He also served Gloucestershire with huge distinction from 1984 until the end of last summer. Showed against Australia this spring that he is far from past it, deep into his 37th year. Is also closing in fast on Kapil Dev's Test wicket record of 434 - he has 411. He has played in close to 200 one-day internationals as well as 108 Tests and became the highest wicket-taker in West Indian history when he went past Malcolm Marshall's 376-mark in South Africa last autumn. He and Curtly Ambrose seem to keep each other going as they defy the years.

STUART WILLIAMS

RHB
Born 12 August 1969

Has struggled to forge himself a Test career, but is now an experienced hand at the one-day international game with more than 50 appearances to his name. An opening batsman with an aggressive approach, Williams' Test debut at Antigua in early 1994, against England, was overshadowed by Brian Lara's world record 375. Born in Nevis, like Arthurton, and a stalwart of the Leeward Islands team. Made his one-day debut in 1994-95, against India at Faridabad, near Delhi. Particularly strong through the offside, but also has been often worried by deliveries moving away from him.

Umpires

by Pat Gibson

DARRELL HAIR

Australia
Born 30 September 1952

Still officially recognised as Australia's top umpire, despite his involvement in the controversy surrounding Sri Lanka off-spinner Muttiah Muralitharan after he called ...m for throwing. A first-class umpire since 1988, he ...as appointed to the international panel in 1994 and ...ade his first appearance in England during the Test ...ries against India in 1996, partnering a tearful Dickie ...ird on his farewell appearance at Lord's. He never ...ayed first-class cricket but was good enough to play for ...vo of Sydney's top grade sides, North Sydney and ...losman, the club where Allan Border began his career, ... a right-hand batsman and fast bowler. He works as a ...les manager for a promotions company and is ...terested in golf, rugby union and horse racing. He also ...sses on his umpiring experience as an officer with the ...ew South Wales training and technical committee.

DAVID SHEPHERD

England
Born 27 December 1940

England's foremost umpire since Dickie Bird retired from international cricket. He is standing in his fifth World Cup, having officiated in 1983, when all the umpires were English, 1987, 1992 and 1996. A middle-order batsman, he played for his native Devon in the Minor Counties before joining Gloucestershire, for whom he is the only player to have scored a century on his first-class debut. He went on to score more than 10,000 runs, including 12 centuries. He became an umpire in 1981, quickly endearing himself to spectators with his superstition of "Nelson" (scores of 111, 222 etc), which has him hopping about on one leg, and was promoted to the Test panel four years later. Along with Bird and Steve Bucknor, he took part in the pilot scheme which led to the formation of the international panel. At home in North Devon he helps his brother run the village post office and, for a hobby, collects stamps.

PETER WILLEY

England
Born 6 December 1949

A former England all-rounder who was appointed to the international panel after only three years on the first-class umpires' list. His first assignment in 1996 was in the ...aribbean which was a fitting starting-point for a ...ombative cricketer who won 15 of his 26 England ...aps against the West Indies when they were the most ...timidating opponents in the world. Born and raised ... County Durham, he became the youngest player to ...ppear for Northamptonshire when he made his debut ...gainst Cambridge University at 16. He played for ...orthants for 18 years before moving to Leicestershire ...or another eight seasons. He finished his career with ...4,361 runs, including 44 centuries, at an average of ...0.56, 756 wickets at 30.95 and 235 catches. He now ...escribes himself as a house-husband and dog-walker.

SRINIVAS VENKATARAGHAVAN

India
Born 21 April 1946

Universally known as Venkat, he was uniquely qualified to join the international panel in 1994, only three years after becoming a first-class umpire. He had already filled just about every other role in Test cricket as player, captain, selector, manager, match referee, television and radio commentator and sports writer. Not surprisingly, he quickly established himself as one of the best umpires in the world and stood in the 1996 World Cup on the sub-continent. A right-hand batsman and off spinner, he played for India in 57 Tests, scoring 894 runs and taking 157 wickets. He toured England four times and also had three seasons in county cricket with Derbyshire. Away from the game, he is an engineering graduate who now works as an industrial marketing consultant. He also plays hockey, badminton and snooker, collects coins and enjoys music.

STEVE DUNNE

New Zealand
Born 22 April 1943

Now New Zealand's senior umpire, he was one of the original members of the international panel and has already stood in two World Cups – in 1992 in Australia and New Zealand and 1996 in India, Pakistan and Sri Lanka. A right hand batsman and left arm fast medium bowler who was good enough to be picked for the New Zealand Under-23 side, he played for the North East Valley club in Otago for 23 years. He became a first-class umpire in 1980 and has been umpiring Test matches for more than 10 years. He lives near Dunedin at the foot of New Zealand's South Island where his first Test between New Zealand and Pakistan became only the fourth to be abandoned without a ball being bowled because of rain. He used to run his own manufacturing and clothing company. He is interested in all sports but his main hobby is breeding English bulldogs.

DOUG COWIE

New Zealand
Born 2 December 1946

A rugby enthusiast, as you would expect of a New Zealander, and a golfer, but essentially a cricket man for most of his life. A right-hand batsman and off-spin bowler, he played for Canterbury University, Mangonui County and the Northland Minor Association before becoming a first-class umpire in 1984. He was appointed to the international panel in 1996 and stood in the second Test in Wellington that winter when England beat New Zealand to record their first victory overseas for two years. A married man with two daughters, he lives in Auckland and works as divisional manager (software) for a computer products company. He is interested in all sports and enjoys travelling and wine-collecting.

RUDI KOERTZEN

South Africa
Born 26 March 1949

A recent addition to the international panel, having first appeared in Test and one-day international cricket during South Africa's historic series against India in 1992-93, their first on home soil for 23 years. He played for the Despatch and De Beers clubs before becoming a first-class umpire in 1981. Married with two sons and two daughters, he works as a building inspector with the Department of Education, Culture and Sport. He also serves on the executive committee of Eastern Province and is interested in all sports, especially golf and fishing.

DAVID ORCHARD

South Africa
Born 24 June 1948

A former Natal cricketer who became a first-class umpire in 1990. A left-hand batsman and right-arm fast medium bowler, he played for Natal from 1967 until 1978, making a highest score of 110 not out and returning best bowling figures of seven for 90. He came to the fore as an umpire on England's tour of South Africa in 1995-96 and was appointed to the international panel soon afterwards. He runs his own business – Apex Coatings and Allied Agencies – and is interested in angling and bird breeding.

STEVE BUCKNOR

West Indies
Born 31 May 1946

A tall, imposing Jamaican whose stature as an umpire is confirmed by the fact that he has stood in the last two World Cup finals, in Melbourne in 1992 and Lahore in 1996. His first love was football and he played for his country at Under-18 level before becoming a FIFA referee, which led to him taking charge of a World Cup match between El Salvador and Holland. He became a first-class umpire in 1987 and took part in the pilot scheme prior to the introduction of the international panel. He stood in the South Africa v India series in 1992-93 when television replays were used for the first time to adjudicate on line decisions and was the first overseas umpire to stand in a Test in England during the New Zealand series in 1994. He lives in Montego Bay and, when he is not travelling the world on umpiring duties, works as a sports consultant.

IAN ROBINSON

Zimbabwe
Born 11 March 1947

Born at Oxford in England but a long-time resident of Harare where he is now the Zimbabwe Cricket Union's administration manager after more than 30 years working for BP and Shell. He played his cricket for Hatfield Sports Club as an opening batsman and wicketkeeper and became a first-class umpire in 1978. He was one of the original members of the international panel and has stood in the last two World Cups. He is heavily involved in the training of umpires but is also interested in gardening and, like, the rest of his family, all sports. His wife, Joan, played softball for Zimbabwe and gained two cricket coaching certificates while his son, Brad, played cricket for the Zimbabwe schools and Under-19 sides before making his first-class debut in 1995. He also played hockey for Zimbabwe at schoolboy level.

JAVED AKHTAR

Pakistan
Born 21 November 1940

A former Pakistan off spinner who umpired the fifth Test between England and South Africa at Headingley last year. He had won his only Test cap on the same ground in 1962 after being flown in as a replacement but it did not turn out to be a happy experience. He failed to take a wicket and scored 2 and 2 not out as Pakistan went down by an innings and 117 runs. He has fonder memories of a match against the MCC at Rawalpindi a year earlier when he took seven for 56, his best bowling figures. He had a highest score of 88 in a career which stretched from 1959 until 1976, bringing him 835 runs at 15.75 and 187 wickets at 18.21. He started umpiring in 1969 and stood in a one-day international on England's last tour of Pakistan in 1987-88 but he was not appointed to the international panel until 1997.

K T FRANCIS

Sri Lanka
Born 15 October 1939

Kandiah Thirugnanasampandapillai Francis, to give him his full name, which explains why they call him KT, is one of the most experienced umpires in the world. He used to work for Sri Lanka Railway and played for the Railway Sports Club as right hand batsman and medium pace bowler before becoming a first-class umpire in 1975. He stood in Sri Lanka's inaugural Test against England in Colombo in 1982 and was one of the first umpires to be appointed to the international panel in 1994. In between times, he had gained a wealth of experience by umpiring all over the world, including England where he stood in the Surrey League for three years and the Village Championship Final at Lords in 1989. His other interests include football, tennis, reading and country and western music.

Referees
by Pat Gibson

JOHN REID

New Zealand
Born 3 June 1928

The best all-rounder New Zealand had ever had until Sir Richard Hadlee embarked on his record-breaking career. A powerful right-hand batsman, a fast medium bowler, a superb fielder and a competent wicketkeeper, he once held every New Zealand record – most Tests, most runs, most centuries, most wickets, most catches and most appearances as captain. He was a fixture in the New Zealand side between 1949 and 1965, playing in 58 consecutive Tests, then a world record. He was captain in 34 of them and led his country to their first three Test victories. In all, he scored 3,428 Test runs, including six centuries, took 85 wickets, held 43 catches and made one stumping. Awarded the OBE for his services to cricket, he went to South Africa to coach Northern Transvaal but had returned to New Zealand when cricket called him again as a match referee.

TALAT ALI

Pakistan
Born 29 May 1950

A former Pakistan opening batsman who became chairman of his board's disciplinary committee in 1996 and first officiated as an international match referee in the West Indies a year later. Dennis Lillee broke his thumb on his debut against Australia at Adelaide in 1972-73 but he returned to bat one-handed in the second innings and went on to play nine more Tests, finishing with 370 runs, including a highest score of 61 against New Zealand at Christchurch. He had toured England in 1971 without playing a Test but had a full home series against England in 1972-73 and appeared in two Tests here in 1978. His first-class career with Lahore, Punjab University, PIA and United Bank stretched from 1967 until 1979 and brought him more than 7,000 runs, including 15 centuries. He is now passenger sales manager for Pakistan International Airlines, plays tennis and enjoys music and reading.

PETER VAN DER MERWE

South Africa
Born 14 March 1937

One of the first match referees to be appointed by the International Cricket Council in 1992. He was originally a slow left arm bowler but it was as a shrewd, bespectacled captain of South Africa who batted solidly down the order that he made his mark in Test cricket. He was captain in eight of his 15 Tests between 1963 and 1967, leading his country to significant victories over M J K Smith's England side in 1965 and Bobby Simpson's Australians in 1966-67. He had emerged from the University of Cape Town to captain both Western Province and Eastern Province in a career which brought him 4,086 runs, including four centuries, and 82 wickets. A chartered accountant, he held directorships with several leading companies before setting up his own financial consultancy business but continued to play a leading role in cricket administration. He was convenor of selectors from 1986 until 1992.

RANJAN MADUGALLE

Sri Lanka
Born 22 April 1959

A former captain of Sri Lanka who quickly established himself as one of the most respected match referees in international cricket, officiating in the last World Cup on the sub-continent in 1996. Originally an off spinner, he developed into a top-class batsman and had already toured England twice with Sri Lanka by the time they made their entry into Test cricket in 1981-82. He introduced himself to Keith Fletcher's side that winter with 142 not out for the President's XI in his home town of Kandy and went on to make 65 in the inaugural Test in Colombo. He was in the Sri Lanka side throughout their first five years in Test cricket and, after a dip in form cost him his place, returned to captain them between 1987 and 1989. Now a marketing consultant, he has served on various committees with the Sri Lanka Cricket Board and been a national selector.

CAMMIE SMITH
West Indies
Born 27 July 1933

A regular visitor to England as a match referee. He brings almost half a century's experience to the job, having been involved in first-class cricket as a player or administrator ever since he made his debut for Barbados in 1951. A tall, forceful opening batsman and occasional wicketkeeper, he scored, 2,277 runs, including five centuries, at an average of 37. He played in five Test matches for the West Indies, four of them on the 1960-61 tour of Australia when he opened with Conrad Hunte and made his highest Test score of 55 at Sydney. His other Test was against India at Port-of-Spain in 1962 when he kept wicket after Jackie Hendriks had broken a finger. He also came to England to play league cricket for Blackpool. Once his playing days were over, he turned to administration, rising to president of the Barbados Cricket Association. He has also served on the West Indies Cricket Board and managed various touring teams.

RAMAN SUBBA ROW
England
Born 29 January 1932

A former England batsman who became one of cricket's leading administrators. A left-hand batsman and leg-break bowler, he played for Cambridge University, Surrey and Northamptonshire, captaining them from 1958 until 1961 and making their highest score of 300 – against Surrey at the Oval. Capped 13 times, he scored 984 Test runs, including three centuries, at an average of 46.85. He retired at 29 to become managing director of a public relations company but remained heavily involved in the game as a member of the MCC committee (1965-68), chairman of the Test and County Cricket Board marketing committee (1969-73), chairman of Surrey (1974-79) and finally chairman of the TCCB itself (1985-1990). He was among the first ICC match referees to be appointed in 1992 and officiated during the 1966 World Cup in India, Pakistan and Sri Lanka.

PETER BURGE
Australia
Born 17 May 1932

A tall, powerful Queenslander who batted with courage and conviction in his 42 Tests for Australia and has brought the same qualities to the role of match referee. An accountant by profession, he had to overcome some prejudice at the start of his playing career because his father was a leading cricket administrator and managed his first tour to the West Indies in 1955. Burge junior soon convinced everyone that he had been chosen on merit with the quality of his batting, which was to bring him 2,290 Test runs at an average approaching 40. He was at his best in Ashes series, scoring all four of his Test centuries against England and producing three of his most memorable performances in this country. He swept Australia to a five-wicket victory at Lord's in 1961, finished that series with 181 at the Oval and then in 1964 changed the course of the Headingley Test with a magnificent 160.

ICC Cricket
WorldCup
England 99

BIGGEST WINNING MARGINS

202 runs	England beat India	Lord's	1975
196 runs	England beat East Africa	Edgbaston	1975
192 runs	Pakistan beat Sri Lanka	Trent Bridge	1975
191 runs	West Indies beat Sri Lanka	Karachi	1987
181 runs	New Zealand beat East Africa	Edgbaston	1975
10 wkts	India beat East Africa	Headingley	1976
10 wkts	West Indies beat Zimbabwe	Edgbaston	1983
10 wkts	West Indies beat Pakistan	Melbourne	1991/92

HIGHEST TEAM TOTALS

398 for 5	Sri Lanka v Kenya	Kandy	1995/96
360 for 4	West Indies v Sri Lanka	Karachi	1987/88
338 for 5	Pakistan v Sri Lanka	Swansea	1983
334 for 4	England v India	Lord's	1975
333 for 9	England v Sri Lanka	Taunton	1983
330 for 6	Pakistan v Sri Lanka	Trent Bridge	1975
328 for 3	South Africa v Holland	Rawalpindi	1995/96
328 for 5	Australia v Sri Lanka	The Oval	1975
322 for 6	England v New Zealand	The Oval	1983
321 for 2	South Africa v UAE	Rawalpindi	1995/96

Gary Kirsten

Sachin Tendulkar

LOWEST TEAM TOTALS

45	Canada v England	Old Trafford	1979
74	Pakistan v England	Adelaide	1991/92
86	Sri Lanka v West Indies	Old Trafford	1975
93	England v Australia	Headingley	1975
93	West Indies v Kenya	Pune	1995/96
94	East Africa v England	Edgbaston	1975
105	Canada v Australia	Edgbaston	1979
120	East Africa v India	Headingley	1975
125	England v Zimbabwe	Albury	1991/92
129	Australia v India	Chelmsford	1983

BEST BATTING

Gary Kirsten	188*	South Africa v UAE	Rawalpindi	1995/96
Viv Richards	181	West Indies v Sri Lanka	Karachi	1987/88
Kapil Dev	175*	India v Zimbabwe	Tunbridge W	1983
Glenn Turner	171*	New Zealand v East Africa	Edgbaston	1975
Andrew Hudson	161	South Africa v Holland	Rawalpindi	1995/96
Aravinda de Silva	145	Sri Lanka v Kenya	Kandy	1995/96
David Houghton	142	Zimbabwe v New Zealand	Hyderabad	1987/88
Viv Richards	138*	West Indies v England	Lord's	1979
Dennis Amiss	137	England v India	Lord's	1975
Sachin Tendulkar	137	India v Sri Lanka	Delhi	1995/96

LEADING ALL-TIME BATSMEN

		Runs	Matches
Javed Miandad	(Pakistan)	1083	33
Viv Richards	(West Indies)	1013	23
Graham Gooch	(England)	897	21
Martin Crowe	(New Zealand)	880	21
Desmond Haynes	(West Indies)	854	25
Arjuna Ranatunga	(Sri Lanka)	835	25
David Boon	(Australia)	815	16
Sachin Tendulkar	(India)	806	15
Aravinda de Silva	(Sri Lanka)	724	20
Ramiz Raja	(Pakistan)	700	16

LEADING ALL-TIME FIELDERS
(excluding wicket-keepers)

		Catches	Matches
Clive Lloyd	(West Indies)	12	17
Desmond Haynes	(West Indies)	12	25
Kapil Dev	(India)	12	26
Lance Cairns	(New Zealand)	10	11
Ian Botham	(England)	10	22
Allan Border	(Australia)	10	25
Javed Miandad	(Pakistan)	10	33
Sanath Jayasuriya	(Sri Lanka)	9	12
Allan Lamb	(England)	9	19
Viv Richards	(West Indies)	9	23

LEADING ALL-TIME BOWLERS

		Wickets	Matches
Imran Khan	(Pakistan)	34	26
Ian Botham	(England)	30	22
Phillip DeFreitas	(England)	29	22
Wasim Akram	(Pakistan)	28	22
Kapil Dev	(India)	26	26
Craig McDermott	(Australia)	27	17
Mushtaq Ahmed	(Pakistan)	26	15
Andy Roberts	(West Indies)	26	16
Abdul Qadir	(Pakistan)	24	13
Manoj Prabhakar	(India)	24	19

LEADING ALL-TIME DISMISSALS
(wicket-keepers)

		Dismissals	Matches
Wasim Bari	(Pakistan)	22	14
Ian Healy	(Australia)	21	14
Jeff Dujon	(West Indies)	20	14
Rod Marsh	(Australia)	18	11
Kiran More	(India)	18	14
Deryck Murray	(West Indies)	16	9
Dave Richardson	(South Africa)	15	9
Syed Kirmani	(India)	14	8
David Williams	(West Indies)	14	8
Moin Khan	(Pakistan)	14	10

Paul Strang

BEST BOWLING

Winston Davis	7/51	West Indies v Australia	Headingley	1983
Gary Gilmour	6/14	Australia v England	Headingley	1975
Ken Macleay	6/39	Australia v India	Trent Bridge	1983
Alan Hurst	5/21	Australia v Canada	Edgbaston	1979
Paul Strang	5/21	Zimbabwe v Kenya	Patna	1995/96
Richard Hadlee	5/25	New Zealand v Sri Lanka	Bristol	1983
Shaukat Dukanwala	5/29	UAE v Holland	Lahore	1995/96
Ashantha de Mel	5/32	Sri Lanka v New Zealand	Derby	1983
Dennis Lillee	5/34	Australia v Pakistan	Headingley	1975
Damien Fleming	5/36	Australia v India	Bombay	1995/96

HIGHEST PARTNERSHIPS FOR EACH WICKET

186	Gary Kirsten/Andrew Hudson	SAF v Hol	Rawalpindi	1995/96
176	Dennis Amiss/Keith Fletcher	Eng v Ind	Lord's	1975
207	Mark Waugh/Steve Waugh	Aus v Ken	V'khapatnam	1995/96
168	Lee Germon/Chris Harris	NZ v Aus	Madras	1995/96
145*	Andy Flower/Andrew Waller	Zim v Sri	N Plymouth	1991/92
144	Imran Khan/Shahid Mahboob	Pak v Sri	Headingley	1983
75*	Duncan Fletcher/Ian Butchart	Zim v Aus	Trent Bridge	1983
117	David Houghton/Ian Butchart	Zim v NZ	Hyderabad	1987/88
126*	Kapil Dev/Syned Kirmani	Ind v Zim	T Wells	1983
71	Andy Roberts/Joel Garner	WI v Ind	Old Trafford	1983

THE ORGANISERS OF THE 1999 CRICKET WORLD CUP WISH TO THANK ALL OF ITS GLOBAL PARTNERS AND OFFICIAL SUPPORTERS

GLOBAL PARTNERS

OFFICIAL SUPPLIERS

The village green joins cricket's carnival

David Hopps doubles as a *Guardian* cricket writer - and as the long-suffering captain of a Yorkshire village cricket team - Thorner Mexborough C.C. Here, he reports on how the team is preparing - in its own inimitable way - for this summer's forthcoming 'Carnival of Cricket' - the 1999 Cricket World Cup.

I n an idle moment today, see if you can spot a dozen empty seats in one of the cheaper parts of the ground. Like as not they will be the ones bought by Thorner Mexborough Cricket Club. When I last heard, the intention was that everybody would be there. But when you try to organise a bunch of Yorkshire village cricketers, it's best to be prepared for the worst.

I'm not knocking the lads, far from it. I'm sure that the 'Thorner Empowered for The Millennium' season will already be proving a huge success (although the title was definitely not my idea and, frankly, with my lack of hair these days, I could do without all those jokes about the Millennium Dome). But, the fact is, it's taken the best part of ten years to get the fielders to walk in together, and that is probably about as much unity as we can handle for one season.

This summer we've had quite enough problems getting into our own cricket ground, never mind the World Cup. In previous seasons, this feat has involved nothing more taxing than opening a rickety old gate, rattling across a cattle grid, and crossing a small field, taking care not to mow down the two horses which represent its only occupants. Total time: one-and-a-half minutes.

This, though, is the age of the communal sports facility – and we have new, security-conscious neighbours. After a gap of about 20

Village cricket

years, the football club have reappeared, and they have announced their presence by ploughing up the field for reseeding, something they could have achieved more easily had they just fed our family of moles a few poppers and persuaded them to tunnel around all night a few yards to the north. To protect their reseeded surface, the football club has erected a barbed-wire fence, complete with a padlocked gate, which, even armed with the necessary keys, would have kept Steve McQueen at bay for a lifetime. When Grenville popped up to the field to mend a slate on our pavilion the other week, he had still not navigated the perimeter fencing when it was time for him to go home for lunch.

Perhaps getting into the World Cup will have proved easier, as long as the guys remembered not to do anything too extravagant. Once in the ground, though, the natural laws of confusion will have applied. Ralls and Mary will have met a company director and his wife, up for the game from High Wycombe, and will have been invited for scotch salmon and champagne in their hospitality box. Just to prove that not everyone is so lucky, Sam will have discovered that, by chance, the Kippax fast bowler he sledged last season is stewarding his part of the stand and is insisting upon an immediate shave with a cut-throat razor to take account of Lord MacLaurin's well-chronicled distaste of facial hair.

And you know those insanely-grinning faces who appeared in the World Cup advertising campaign? Well, Rabbit will already be down the pub, chatting up the surprised-looking women with the sunflower poking from her straw boater. After all, it's not as if Rabbit doesn't have previous, having travelled all the way to Australia for the Ashes series, and then barely seeing a ball bowled on account of being waylaid by a deliciously buxom surfing trainer from Manly.

Then there is the little matter of transport to the game. It sounded unreliable. That much became certain when someone had the bright idea of cadging lifts from the parents of our defunct U13 side, which collapsed because the parents proved themselves useless when asked to transport their own kids to the occasional cricket match. We would have been better advised to travel by Richard Branson's hot-air balloon, especially as by tethering it alongside the boundary we could have offered an appealing advertising opportunity for our match-ball sponsors.

 We would have been better advised to travel by Richard Branson's hot-air balloon.

The attempt at running a junior side was not all bad, though. I'm sure that the parents were secretly very grateful for our Free Baby-Sitting Service, and the £1 subs that we requested but rarely received had probably just fallen through an inconvenient hole in a trouser pocket. We should have thought to offer a Free Sewing Service while we were at it. It was the night that

Ben Hollioak

one of the parents asked us to "make Robin's tea, and would you mind awfully helping him with his science homework before popping him off to bed?" which brought it home to us that our attempts to foster a feeling of Sport in the Community was not exactly going to plan. You might well spot a parent of one of our juniors today. Just look out for the posh one, thoughtfully advising a steward that she'll be back around eight to pick up Jonathan, who needs to take the yellow tablet once an hour, the blue tablet if he starts coughing and the cream whenever the sun comes out.

Still, mustn't grumble! It's the World Cup! The Carnival of Cricket! As Gibbo, our hyper-active captain, points out, if we want to be "among the elite for the new millennium" (that's the first division of the Wetherby & District Cricket League to the uninitiated), there is so much we can learn to fuel our promotion challenge when the World Cup comes to town. He has suggested that we should watch every match with pen and paper at hand, noting down whatever useful tips we have gleaned for the rest of the summer. I am following his advice and ave so far compiled the following useful list:

They have sightscreens and we don't

They have a scorer and we don't

They always know intuitively where middle-and-leg is and we don't

One thing about the World Cup... it certainly brings a bit of fun when it comes to betting. We've been holding sweepstakes on the tournament for months now. I've not had the best of luck. Among the tickets I have drawn in the past few months are ones proclaiming that Adam Hollioake would be named as England captain, that Ben Hollioake would be the star of the tournament, and that Matthew Fleming and Dougie Brown would both be named in England's fifteen. I was quite optimistic at first, all three of these predictions having been made in ECB's official guide, Cricket 98. It is nice to reflect that officialdom was as deluded as the rest of us, but the fact is that I'm £3 down on the deal. This is to add to the hundreds of pounds that disappear annually into the fund-raising black hole otherwise known as the Thorner 200 Club. I wouldn't say that Carol and Denis run the 200 Club on fear, but I am still paying monthly contributions for several distant relations who have been dead for years.

> **❛ Talk about confusion in the ranks. ❜**

But we began by talking about 'walking-in', as I recall. In one of our captain's more morbid moments, I suggested to Gibbo that he should adopt the phraseology of George Graham, when he coaches Tottenham Hotspur's defenders. "Imagine you're on a rope," George tells his troops. "You're all connected – when one of you does something, the rest must follow." And with this simple advice, they immediately turn into one of the meanest defences that English football has ever known.

It also works quite well in cricket, we have since discovered, and it was perfectly understandable that, in his mindless enthusiasm, Gibbo became somewhat confused and assumed

that we had to use a real rope. By the time we had untangled the knots, the pubs were calling last orders.

And then, would you believe it, the following week, Peasy (in a thirst for religious insight naturally given to a former scout master) chanced upon that biography about Jonty Rhodes. Would you believe it! In among all the stuff about thanking the Lord for all his achievements, the World's Greatest Fielder reveals that he doesn't much believe in walking in, but instead imagines himself standing in the covers like a soccer goalkeeper. Talk about confusion in the ranks! The only player who looked happy at this information was Wakker, who has imagined himself to be Alan Hansen for years and can now justify those languid interceptions with his boot as being a fielding technique ahead of its time. •

David Hopps, former cricket correspondent of The Yorkshire Post and for the past decade a sportswriter with The Guardian, was short-listed for the William Hill Sports Book of the Year Award 1998. His book 'We're Right Behind You, Captain!' covered England's tribulations as well as his own trials as captain of Thorner Mexborough CC in the Wetherby and District Cricket League. Like Mike Atherton, he has since resigned.

Jonty Rhodes

Tournament Format

Group Matches

Each team will play every other team in its group. Points will be allocated for each Win, Tie or No Result in accordance with the system described below, which will apply throughout the Tournament.

Following the Group Matches the top three teams from each group will progress to the next phase, the Super Six. The teams will be placed in order of merit based on the points gained in the Group Matches and will take forward into the Super Six phase the points scored against the other teams which have qualified from their group.

In the Super Six phase of competition, each of the three qualifying teams from Group A will play each of the three qualifying teams from Group B.

The top four teams at the end of the Super Six phase of the competition will progress to the Semi-finals where the team placed first will play the team placed fourth and the team placed second will play the team placed third.

The winners of the Semi-finals will contest the Final.

Duration

All matches will consist of one innings per side, and each innings will be limited to 50 six-ball overs. A minimum of 25 overs per team will constitute a match. Matches will be of one day's scheduled duration with one reserve day allocated (two reserve days in the case of the Final). The reserve day(s) will be used if necessary to continue a match which has not been completed on the first scheduled day.

Scheduled Start and Cessation Times

The scheduled hours of play will be 10.45am to 6.30pm. If there is a delayed start or one or more interruptions in play, the Umpires may order extra time on the first day if they consider that a result can be obtained on that day. If the Umpires are satisfied that a result cannot be obtained on the first day, the timing for the cessation of play on that day will be 8.00pm, subject to conditions of ground, weather and light.

Session of Play and Interval between Innings

There will normally be two sessions of play of 3 hours 30 minutes each, separated by an interval of 45 minutes between 2.15pm and 3.00pm.

Length of Innings

(i) Uninterrupted Matches

(i.e. Matches Which Are Neither Delayed Nor Interrupted)

Each team shall bat for 50 (six ball) overs unless all out

earlier. A team shall not be permitted to declare its innings closed.

If the team fielding first fails to bowl the required number overs by the scheduled time for the cessation of the first session, play shall continue until the required number of overs has been bowled.

Unless otherwise determined by the Referee, the innings of the team batting second shall be limited to the same number of overs that it bowled by the scheduled time for the cessation of the first session. The over in progress at the scheduled cessation time shall count as a complete over. The interval shall not be extended and the second session shall commence at the scheduled time (3.00pm).

The Referee may increase the number of overs to be bowled by the team bowling second if, after consultation with the Umpires, he is of the opinion that events beyond the control of the team bowling first prevented that team from bowling the required number of overs by the scheduled time for the cessation of the first innings.

If the team batting first is all out and the last wicket falls at or after the scheduled time for the interval, the innings of the team batting second shall be limited to the same number of overs bowled to the team batting first at the scheduled time for the interval.

If the team fielding second fails to bowl 50 overs or the number of overs as provided for above by the scheduled cessation time, the hours of play shall be extended until the required number of overs has been bowled or a result achieved.

(ii) Delayed or Interrupted Matches

Any rearrangement of the number of overs that may be necessary due to a delayed start or one or more interruptions in play as a result of adverse ground, weather or light conditions or any other reason, shall only be made on the second day (third day in the case of the Final). The timing and duration of all suspensions of play (including all intervals) or delays on any day will be taken into account when calculating the length of time available for either innings.

The object shall always be to rearrange the number of overs so that, if possible, both teams have the opportunity of batting for the same number of overs.

Restrictions on the Placement of Fieldsmen

Two semi-circles shall be drawn on the field of play. The semi-circles shall have as their centre the middle stump at either end of the pitch. The radius of each of the semi-circles shall be 30 yards (27.5m). The ends of each semi-circle shall be joined to the other by a straight line drawn on the filed on the same side of the pitch. The field restriction area should be marked by continuous painted white lines of 'dots' at five-yard (4.5m) intervals, each 'dot' to be covered

a white plastic or rubber (but not metal) disc measuring
en inches (18cm) in diameter.

the instant of delivery, there may not be more than five
dsmen on the leg side.

r the first 15 overs only two fieldsmen are permitted to be
tside the field restriction marking at the instant of
livery.

r the remaining overs only five fieldsmen are permitted to
outside the field restriction marking at the instant of
livery.

vo inner circles shall be drawn on the field of play. The
cles have as their centres the centre point of the popping
ase at either end of the pitch. The radius of each of the
cles is 15 yards (13.72 metres). The field restriction area
ould be marked by 'dots'. The segment of the circles
served for the slip positions shall not be demarcated.
efer attached Appendix 1).

the first 15 overs there must be a minimum of two
ationary fieldsmen within the 15-yard field restriction of
e striker at the instant of delivery. The two stationary
ldsmen may be permitted to stand deeper than 15 years
the un-demarcated area) provided only that they are
anding in slip, leg slip and gully positions.

umber of Overs Per Bowler

o bowler shall bowl more than 10 overs in an innings.

a delayed or interrupted match where the overs are
duced for both teams or for the team bowling
cond, no bowler may bowl more than one-fifth of
e total overs allowed.

here the total overs are not divisible by five,
e additional over shall be allowed to the
aximum number per bowler necessary to
ake up the balance.

oints

he following points system will apply

Vin	2
ie or No Result	1
oss	0

roup Matches

the event of teams finishing on equal points in either
roup, the right to play in the Super Six stage will be
ecided in the following order of priority:

) The most wins in the Group Matches.

) When two teams have both equal points and equal
wins, the team which was the winner of the Group
Match played between them will be placed in the
higher position.

When more than two teams have equal points and
equal wins, the team which was the winner of the most
number of matches played between those teams will be
placed in the higher position.

(c) If still equal, the team with the higher net run rate in
the Group Matches will be placed in the higher
position (excludes matches when the Duckworth/Lewis
method is used).

(d) If still equal, the team with the higher number of
wickets taken per balls bowled in the Group Matches
in which results were achieved, will be placed in the
higher position.

(e) In the highly unlikely event that teams cannot be
separated by (a) to (d) above this will be done by
drawing lots.

Super Six Matches

The six teams that qualify for the Super Six stage carry forward
the points that they have gained against the other teams that
have qualified from their respective groups. The points
carried forward by each team are added to those they gain in
the Super Six Matches, to form the Super Six league table.

In the event of teams finishing on equal points at the end of
the Super Six stage, the right to play in the Semi-final will
be decided in the following order of priority:

(a) The most wins in all of the matches throughout the
competition against the other Super Six qualifiers.

(b) When two teams have both equal points and equal wins,
the team which was the winner of the match played
between them (in either the Group or Super Six
Matches) will be placed in the higher position.

When more than two teams have equal points and
equal wins, the team which was the winner of the
most number of matches played between
those teams (in both the Group and the
Super Six Matches) will be placed in the
higher position.

(c) If still equal, the team with the higher net run
rate in all matches played against the other Super Six
qualifiers (in both the Group and Super Six Matches) will
be placed in the higher position.

(d) If still equal, the team with the higher number of
wickets taken per balls bowled in all of the matches
throughout the competition against the other Super Six
qualifiers in which results were achieved, will be placed in
the higher position.

(e) In the highly unlikely event that teams cannot be
separated by (a) to (d) above this will be done by drawing
lots.

Semi-final

If a Semi-final is tied or there is no result, the team that
finished higher at the end of the Super Six stage shall
proceed to the Final.

Final

In the event of a tied Final or if there is no result in the
three days allocated, the World Cup will be shared by the
finalists.

Match Schedule

DATE	MATCH	VENUE	BROADCASTER
Friday May 14	England v Sri Lanka	Lord's	Sky Sports
Saturday May 15	India v South Africa	Hove	Sky Sports
	Zimbabwe v Kenya	Taunton	Sky Sports
Sunday May 16	Australia v Scotland	Worcester	BBC
	West Indies v Pakistan	Bristol	BBC
Monday May 17	New Zealand v Bangladesh	Chelmsford	Sky Sports
Tuesday May 18	England v Kenya	Canterbury	BBC
Wednesday May 19	Sri Lanka v South Africa	Northampton	Sky Sports
	India v Zimbabwe	Leicester	Sky Sports
Thursday May 20	Australia v New Zealand	Cardiff	BBC
	Pakistan v Scotland	Chester-le-Street	BBC
Friday May 21	West Indies v Bangladesh	Ireland	Sky Sports
Saturday May 22	England v South Africa	The Oval	BBC
	Zimbabwe v Sri Lanka	Worcester	BBC
Sunday May 23	Kenya v India	Bristol	Sky Sports
	Australia v Pakistan	Headingley	Sky Sports
Monday May 24	West Indies v New Zealand	Southampton	BBC
	Scotland v Bangladesh	Edinburgh	BBC
Tuesday May 25	England v Zimbabwe	Trent Bridge	Sky Sports
Wednesday May 26	Sri Lanka v India	Taunton	BBC
	South Africa v Kenya	Amstelveen	BBC
Thursday May 27	West Indies v Scotland	Leicester	Sky Sports
	Australia v Bangladesh	Chester-le-Street	Sky Sports
Friday May 28	New Zealand v Pakistan	Derby	Sky Sports
Saturday May 29	England v India	Edgbaston	Sky Sports
	Zimbabwe v South Africa	Chelmsford	Sky Sports
Sunday May 30	Sri Lanka v Kenya	Southampton	BBC
	West Indies v Australia	Old Trafford	BBC
Monday May 31	Scotland v New Zealand	Edinburgh	Sky Sports
	Pakistan v Bangladesh	Northampton	Sky Sports
	SUPER SIX		
Friday June 4	Group A 2nd v Group B 2nd	The Oval	Sky Sports
Saturday June 5	Group A 1st v Group B 1st	Trent Bridge	BBC
Sunday June 6	Group A 3rd v Group B 3rd	Headingley	Sky Sports
Tuesday June 8	Group A 2nd v Group B 1st	Old Trafford	Sky Sports
Wednesday June 9	Group A 3rd v Group B 2nd	Lord's	BBC
Thursday June 10	Group A 1st v Group B 3rd	Edgbaston	Sky Sports
Friday June 11	Group A 3rd v Group B 1st	The Oval	BBC
Saturday June 12	Group A 2nd v Group B 3rd	Trent Bridge	BBC
Sunday June 13	Group A 1st v Group B 2nd	Headingley	Sky Sports
	SEMI-FINALS		
Wednesday June 16	Team 1 v Team 4	Old Trafford	BBC
Thursday June 17	Team 2 v Team 3	Edgbaston	Sky Sports
	THE FINAL		
Sunday June 20		Lord's	BBC Sky Sports

1999 Cricket World Cup Ticket Centre 0870 606 1999 (calls charged at national rate)
Lines open from 9.00am until 5.30pm weekdays. Tickets also available from your local First Class County Club